the art of
.COMbat

the art of
.COMbat

ANCIENT WISDOM FOR THE COMPETITIVE ECONOMY

Shawn P. McCarthy

John Wiley & Sons, Inc.
New York · Chichester · Weinheim · Brisbane · Singapore · Toronto

The edition of Sun Tzu's *The Art of War* quoted herein was translated from the Chinese by Lionel Giles (1910) and is available on the Project Gutenberg (University of Illinois–Urbana) Web site.

Quote from Seymour Cray used by permission, NewMediaTV.com and KRON-TV, San Jose. Statistics on Internet use by purchasing managers used by permission from a study conducted by *Purchasing* magazine, fall 1999. Quote from *Burn Rate: How I Survived the Gold Rush Years on the Internet* by Michael Wolff, used by permission of Simon & Schuster, Inc. Statistics from studies on e-marketplaces, including "The Demise of Dot Com Retailers," quoted from Forrester Research, with permission.

This book is printed on acid-free paper. ∞

ISBN 0-471-41519-7

Printed in the United States of America.

10 9 8 7 6 5 4 3 2 1

To my wife Karen,
for all her support

contents

acknowledgments

Many people helped lighten the load for this book. At the risk of forgetting someone, I do want to thank those who made researching, writing, editing, and presenting this book an enjoyable experience.

Thanks to my kids, Danny and Kelly, for giving up their daddy for too many evenings and weekends.

Thanks to Terra Lycos for its support. In particular, thanks to Kathy O'Reilly in the Terra Lycos marketing department, Jeff Snider in the legal department, and Jane Emerson of the Lycos Kids Channel. A special thanks to former Terra Lycos president of U.S. operations (now CEO of Ellacoya Networks), Ron Sege, for his market insights.

Thanks to my editor, Airie Dekidjiev, for her ability to find focus and clarity in the text I threw at her, and helping me expand on basic ideas.

Thanks to all the CEOs of small companies and budding venture capitalists that I cornered, tape recorder in hand, and places like Internet World, ISPCon, and other conventions whose wisdom and experience I drew upon during a very volatile market time.

Thanks to Tom Temin and Susan Menke of Government Computer News & Post Newsweek Business Tech Media Group for believing in my abilities as a tech writer and eventually as a Web site developer many years ago, which started me down this path.

And finally, thanks to my parents, Mary and Jack, and sisters, Debbie, Laurel, and Eileen, for inspiring a lifelong fascination with exploring and learning, both online and off.

introduction

In 500 B.C., General Sun Tzu wrote the highly influential book *The Art of War,* which offered a framework for waging war and valuable observations on the nature of battle. So important was this text that over the millennia it's been translated into many languages, updated and adapted to describe everything from the internal workings of sales processes to investment strategies to modern politics. In *The Art of .combat,* I am not adapting Sun Tzu's text to a new context. Rather, I'm creating a new approach for understanding the concepts while disassembling the framework of his lessons, and reconstructing them over modern e-commerce systems and Internet-based business. Less than 5 percent of the original text by Sun Tzu remains in this volume and only those rules and theories that are still relevant, albeit transformed, are included. *The Art of .combat* is an entirely new way of understanding the internal workings and competitive nature of the e-world and operating within its complex landscape. This book shows the subtleties of the terrain through examples from the current e-business world, including firsthand experiences from Lycos.

In *The Art of War,* Sun Tzu describes Chinese weapons, ancient command and communications systems, discipline, grade distinctions, strategy, and logistics. He also provides very specific details about equipment and costs that are irrelevant today. For example, he explains how to use chariots, minutiae on how many gold pieces must be laid out in order to move an army across a great distance, and when soldiers should be executed. War has changed a great deal since the time of Sun Tzu. You don't see a lot of chariots, shields, or swords in modern warfare, and even fewer in business deals. Battle strategies and goals have changed, too, but some of the basic methods to assess and manage competition and conflict remain relevant. Simple rules like observing before planning, planning before moving, and being able to switch plans quickly still hold true. The importance of financial backing and taking care of your soldiers (or employees) has not changed, even though the weapons of battle, the battle itself, and the people have changed greatly. On the whole, *The Art of .combat* offers a new way of understanding and managing the cutthroat context of the new economy, the internal structure of the new company, the urgency of new customer demands, and the new economy's fiercely competitive climate. The end result is the new rules of .combat.

One of the concepts explored is how to utilize the Internet to the most effective end. At least one CEO of a top e-commerce site says the Net is a tool, not a market to be won. It's the most powerful new business tool in recent history, and finding ways to use it is an art unto itself. In this book, I sort out the best of the e-business world's proven lessons about strategy, offering examples and details on how tactics can be applied. The new framework will guide you through assessing the landscape, strategizing against or with the competition, doing battle while keeping your long-term goals in place, and understanding the infrastructure of this new terrain. Truth be told, the war for online dominance is really a series of battles for every type of market space there is. It is up to you to decide which space you want to grab hold of, and you need to understand the larger picture of where that market fits within the online world. There will be no one clear winner across the entire Net. Being the top traffic portal is not even a clear path toward online dominance. Just as there is no single world ruler, there will be no one master of the Internet.

It may surprise some readers to know that Sun Tzu was not a man who admired war. He thought the best war is that which is won before the battle is ever fought—because the opponent knows he will lose. More is lost than won in fighting just for the sake of fighting. Through knowledge of one's opponent, and through detailed planning, an advantage is gained from the start. If both sides do their homework, both sides will realize who has the advantage, and an outright battle can be avoided.

Leadership in the e-world is equally important as proper planning and carries its own unique set of qualifications. Trust and respect are paramount, but so is an understanding of the unique nature of online business development. Employees need to know their leader is capable of competing in this space. Sun Tzu had a profound respect for other leaders, even his enemies, and had an understanding of and empathy for their goals. He believed there is a certain nobility in fighting for what one believes in, even when referring to the opposition. Yet despite this compassion, he was also a tough commander who demanded discipline in his troops, even to the point where he would execute those who might disobey and hinder the army's mission. Today, the duality of his approach is considered paradoxical. In ancient times, he was considered tough and wise.

Today, the role of leader as manager of change is especially crucial. The importance of sparking innovation and the ability to quickly adapt key new technologies has proven important time and time again. The first army to face a motorized tank on the battlefield could tell you how important it is to adopt innovative technologies as fast as your opponent. So could the first navy to confront an iron fighting ship, or the first army to face a bomber.

However, other concepts differ online. In the online world, time and distance are compressed to the point where distance isn't as central an issue as it once was. But being aware of your competition on a global scale is key. There are new workplace issues for the new leader to consider as well. In the age of venture capital and stock options for employees, keeping your workers satisfied means thoroughly understanding what they need and want. This demands knowledge of the modern transformed worker who has been enabled by technology, and even the financial structure enabling workers to make new choices.

Within the structure of the Internet economy, an understanding of the rules of engagement in the virtual marketplace determines who comes out on top. Winners and losers are judged by market share, return on investment, and ownership of key technologies. The Internet is a weapon shared by all, but mastered by the few who know not only how to maneuver within it, but how to best use the weapon.

Winning Factors

In this book, some key concepts resurface. These aren't just buzzwords or phrases. They are the major factors that influence how the Internet is used as a powerful business tool for winning market share. These concepts include:

Understanding that marketplaces are the modern battlefields. The Internet is a strategic weapon toward winning key markets. It is indeed wrong to consider the Internet strictly as a battlefield unto itself. The Net can be many things, including a messenger, a reconnaissance vehicle, a strategic weapon, and a battlefield. There has never been a tool that fills so many different roles in a conflict.

People have changed. In the e-business world, leaders are judged by new criteria. Knowledge has a new role. Employees want and need new tools and new rewards. All the people-motivated functions within business have been transformed.

Creating a new market is the key to controlling a new market. Understanding an existing marketplace is vital to taking it over from its current owner or settling new territory.

Timing is everything. Sometimes winning comes by waiting rather than attacking.

The best products are built using a positive feedback cycle. Changes are evolutionary. Customers will help you create the best product for their business community, and help you take over the market space. In the age of the online relationship between buyer and seller, you have more possibilities for interaction and feedback than ever.

Future market controllers are those who can perfect the supply chain of its customers. The goal is frictionless commerce. Every time product is moved, costs are added. Every time product sits still, it depreciates and commerce opportunities are lost. Those who add value are those who can reduce friction, cutting costs and improving efficiency. Moving data over the Internet, and moving a physical object only at the last possible second, is a prime way to do this. So is proper partnering. Soon, companies won't compete with other companies so much as supply chains will compete with other supply chains.

Unlike real war, in business, sometimes you win by being acquired. Public companies, stock options, and exit strategies have forever changed the landscape. Despite the recent backlash against the in-and-out business strategy for start-up companies, the emergence of the new financial business model, and acknowledgment of the value of first-mover status and market share, will have a continued effect on how we view financial stability and total worth. Built-to-flip has become acceptable in some circumstances.

Alliances, even with competitors, can lead to long-term success. Unlike the wars of yesteryear, businesses can often find win-win situations where both sides gain more than if either side fought for an outright victory. Win-win is not a stalemate. It's a limited partnership in which each side gains a special focus and a synergy that could not be found in separate camps.

There is an evolving marketplace for everything, even your time. People will bid for a moment of your time. Each target demographic will settle into its own price range. Market makers are those who can deliver blocks of specific types of people to those who want to place their message in front of them.

Businesses need to exist, in some form, in the physical world as well as the cyber world. This was a key message from the .com meltdown. New businesses who wish to establish a new market space, and who operate as Internet-only ventures (straight .com companies) face a tough transition from concept phase to demonstration phase to legitimate business phase. The first merger to prove the coexistence of content and distribution was the AOL/Warner merger.

The emergence and effects of global connectedness. The move toward ubiquitous computing and universal Internet access makes online marketplaces much different from traditional marketplaces with regional reach. This is truly a global battle, to the extent that isolationist governments who attempt to limit Net access and maintain local control of their economies will topple.

With these new thresholds and determinants, *The Art of .combat* is far different from *The Art of War*, yet business maneuvering and out-and-out fighting come from the same need—to compete and win. Anyone who enters the modern Internet fray literally has to stand on the shoulders of giants just to see the vast battlefield where they will compete. We should take advantage of the harsh lessons learned by others in the .com world, and use these lessons to build a foundation for future success. General Sun Tzu himself would have told you that understanding the enemy and the battlefield is the first step toward planning for victory.

PART ONE

basic training

appraise yourself, the landscape, and your opposition

You already know much about the basics of the e-business world and how it evolved, if not firsthand, then from watching and hearing about the strategies and stories of countless companies—both Web-based and brick-and-mortar. What is not so intuitive, and therefore requires closer examination, is how Internet *business* operates.

> Whether you are a successful brick-and-mortar company looking to add a Web-based component to your business, or are already operating in the online world, you need to closely examine yourself, the landscape, and the opposition in order to correctly judge how to gain the upper hand and face what is now a fierce fight for the survival of the fittest.

Remind yourself that business is different online and that, in order to make your business succeed, you must know and accept your weaknesses while leveraging your strengths. You must listen to and follow the new rules, understand the new ways of dealing with your competition and the new method to develop your business.

Answer these questions to figure out where you stand in terms of knowledge: Do you understand how content distribution through online partnerships works? Do you know how content and branding opportunities can be traded or purchased to extend your online presence? Do you know how to optimally transform your content into data feeds sent to remote-hosted sites, and make this process pay? Should you pay a slotting fee to feature your company's goods and services on a major Web portal? Is it better to be located in the portal's shopping area, or to have a more ubiquitous presence in specialized search results or vertical content areas? Whether you know the answer to one, all, or none of these questions, you need to dig deeper and learn how to make this consolidating industry work for you, revisiting what you thought you knew. This book shows you the more subtle aspects of making these decisions. In order to understand how the online business environment works, you must take 10 steps backward and survey the whole battle map.

Basic but valuable information includes, for example, the role of search engines and portal sites, and what they are becoming. Other essentials include knowing how market spaces are created online and how they are accessed, and a familiarity with the new currencies that drive this burgeoning economy. Simple examples of innovative business methods include obtaining an equity position in a company you're partnering with, or establishing content distribution mechanisms (i.e., getting your products featured on other people's Web sites). These new methods are sometimes as profitable as traditional product promotions. In-depth examples are outlined later in the book.

This is an environment where everyone does everything; be prepared to wear many hats.

So on we move to the starting point for learning the art of .combat. You are about to embark on authentic basic training. **Know what you *do* know about the fundamentals of technology. Realize what you *don't* know about new business models. And be aware of the huge terrain between the two.**

In this relatively new territory, everyone, from the biggest corporations to the kid next door, has access to the same market space as you. You must pitch your flag and mark your turf as well as understand this terrain consists of fluid boundaries. Your trick is to provide value to your limited tract so you can first insert yourself in the .com traffic and money flow. After that, you can extract your profit.

One sexy cutting edge of the Internet is the entertainment world, with its online video streams, music broadcasts, and networked gaming. This book looks at these businesses and what you can learn and gain from them. In comparison, a study of how product flows to and from any business, online or not, may not seem as exciting, but understanding how the old models have changed is crucial.

Reexamine the Business Model

In a generic sense, businesses obtain raw or refined materials from others, add value to the materials, and then sell them to others. This means, on the most basic level, that all businesses are in the service industry. They provide a service that enhances a product, and other people pay for that service.

A basic example is a mining company that provides a service by removing iron ore from the ground. They then send the ore to a smelter (within the same company, or a separate company) that provides the service of refining the iron into a usable metal. For example, carbon and other elements are added to produce steel. From there, the material is sent to forges, foundries, and factories where other value and services are added along the way. Eventually, the metal ends up as the fender on your car and the fork in your hand.

Steel is a great example of a vertical industry. In a vertical industry, you can track the flow of products from raw material to finished goods. If a shortage develops at any level, all the downstream operations in the vertical industry feel the pinch. If the price of iron ore rises, the price of its products responds in kind all through the vertical.

In any industry, manufacturers are at the mercy of both their up-stream suppliers and downstream customers. This is true even in the entertainment and software industries. What could a movie director accomplish if she couldn't find cameras, film, lights, actors, costumes, production facilities, and a distribution company for the finished product? How could a software developer succeed if he can't find computers, programming tools, technical support, and someone to buy his creations?

No matter what business you're in, think of it as a manufacturing process. Supply and demand exist at every level of every industry. **Today, the larger your scope of supply and demand and your role in it, the better foothold you will have in the e-business world.** No matter what your industry, the Internet is a key tool to broaden that view, redefine your scope, and extend your reach not only to new suppliers and new customers, but to the information they possess about pricing, inventory, and shipping.

"No one yet does this exceptionally well," said Ron Sege, CEO of Ellacoya Networks. "The paragon for this is probably Cisco. It's difficult to do it well because it's tough to get the right philosophical approach among all the participants. The reason Cisco did it well is they had no legacy system, they became big very fast and they could direct their suppliers and control how they would share their data. Wal-Mart is another company that's good at this. Information is power, and being able to share information with your suppliers and distributors, as Wal-Mart and Cisco have done, drives costs down. It makes you more flexible and responsive to your users, which creates more customer satisfaction."

This is what you must do to survive. Learning *how* now, while everyone else is also learning, keeps you in the game. "The competitive imperative will force companies who can afford to do this to move aggressively," Sege said. "Companies who don't move aggressively, because they can't afford it, or because they aren't insightful enough, will be less competitive and will eventually go away."

Look Closer at the *New* Supply Chain Management

Supply chain management (SCM) is a rather dry term for a fairly exciting phenomenon, and its role in the new business revolution is downright thrilling. Every product you touch came from a supply chain. There are many examples besides steel. The paper in a book passes through many businesses and many hands during its production from trees in a forest to paper rolls on a printing press. Magnetic tape in an audiocassette and the plastic case that houses it come from dozens of different starting points. The people who assemble these parts need continuous access to every piece required to build the final product. When a person or machine reaches back to grab the next piece on an assembly line, the piece had better be there.

One key way to add value to a manufacturing process is to analyze a supply chain and squeeze out some costs. Your supermarket does this all the time to shave a few pennies off the cost of apples or milk. That's why you see apples from Washington State one week, then New Zealand the next week. The store's purchasing agents buy in bulk from several sources to play one supplier off the other and keep prices low. You likely see multiple brands of milk, too, but with milk, even big supermarket chains tend to buy from a few local suppliers. Because the product has a shorter shelf life, it's more important for the supermarket to reduce shelf time and spoilage. It's a different sort of cost-cutting measure, which leads me to a key tactic for assessing your business.

Successful businesses must use the Internet to get a much broader view of their supply chain and the inventories of their trading partners, so they can identify new places where costs can be contained.

Progressive businesses increasingly use Net-based tools to control their supply chain. Such duties used to be handled by conscientious purchasing managers. These managers may still track this information, but their talents and duties have changed remarkably. For example, a fall 1999 survey by *Purchasing* magazine showed that 38 percent of purchasing managers now place major orders over the Internet. Also, half of those surveyed who do not presently, planned to start focusing their purchasing via the Net over the next three years. What does this mean for you? It means you must develop a new skill set for gathering and comparing online data, working with online order forms, and using the Web to find new supply sources. Larry R. Smeltzer, professor of supply chain management at Arizona State University's College of Business, recently wrote, "The forthcoming issue will be how to use technology to a strategic advantage. Pushing the buttons is not the issue . . . strategy and competitive advantages will be the focus." For this reason, data gathering and analysis via the Net is fast becoming a required skill for purchasers. The actual purchasing is secondary.

A seismic shift in many roles is the norm; even the role of the storefront has been transformed. In the future, regional retailers may use their stores as service bureaus rather than as sales points. For example, car dealers may only deliver and service autos that are ordered online rather than guiding visitors through car showrooms where they push existing inventory. Local car dealers won't go away, but their duties and profit centers will shift. More of their profits will come from warranty repair work, handling vehicle leasing contracts (and eventually selling the used car once the lease ends), and parts distribution.

A crucial part of analyzing your business is assessing possible future scenarios causing profit centers to shift and the component parts of your business to likewise shift.

New market advantages and disadvantages arise from this shift. Local merchants, for example, won't compete against the price and selection of national online megastores. How could they? They'll never reach the level of volume and discount that the big online merchants can establish. But local stores will continue to enjoy the advantage of proximity. People want the involvement of a local merchant when their products need service. Plus, customers perceive value in the live assistance and personal contact that local businesses provide. There are also cost advantages in the regional location of inventory. A used car for sale down the street may be cheaper than a used car located in another state simply because it doesn't have to be transported to you. Likewise, appliance manufacturers will likely always maintain regional warehouses for their goods so orders can be distributed quickly and efficiently.

Face the Extreme Competition

Virtually any business process involves an exchange of information and some level of product marketing. These are two key functions that the Web was born to handle.

> **Failure to implement a strategy that takes advantage of the communications, commerce, and reach of the Net could be the first step toward ruin for an otherwise successful and prosperous company. Your opponents count on that. They hope you botch this important transition. You must disappoint them.**

No matter what market space you want to carve out, how well-honed your supply chain is, or how perfectly positioned you are in the brick-and-mortar universe, a tremendous amount of competition challenges your move into the online business world. This is especially true as the early waves of online merchants are shaken out through stock-price drops and the consolidation that started in spring 2000. It's survival of the fittest on a vicious battlefield. You're competing with hungry, low-budget operations maintained by stock-option-holding staffers willing to work far into the night. Like the North Vietnamese Army of old, they travel light and are confident they can defeat larger, better-equipped, and more experienced opponents. Why? Because they are willing to work harder, risk more, and do whatever is necessary to succeed, no matter how absurd and futile the effort may seem to others. And, like the North Vietnamese Army, they may never have to face the full fury of their enemy. They may compete with sprawling businesses that are too busy with other interests and projects to focus all time and energy into winning a specific online battle. The single-mindedness of these small, rogue corporations is their greatest asset.

How will you compete with that?

A shrewd understanding of the opponent's motivation, strengths, weaknesses, and needs, an understanding of their supply chain, and yours, and any possible differences, gives you the upper hand.

This is your answer. The competition tactics as laid out by Sun Tzu have now been adapted for battle both offline and online. Wise observers adapted the analytical part of his road map, and understood how to exploit their link in the supply chain, over the length of the industrial age. They were able to see new opportunities as they developed. The Internet is the new tool you must use to capitalize on such information. The Net is the weapon you must use to streamline your own business process.

Armed with this understanding, you can leverage your assets in a way that makes you and your company as productive and efficient as any hungry power user who does his best work in the glow of a computer monitor at 3 A.M.

You are now engaged in battle against a very different sort of opposition that moves over a different sort of battlefield. **To survive, you need a combination of instinct, business skill, technical knowledge, and a good battle plan. But more than anything, you need to know your enemy.**

Assess the Five Factors

After you assess your own strengths, you need to discover the strengths and weaknesses of your opponent, and you need to know the look and feel of the field where you will compete. This is easier than you might think. It's a matter of knowing the right questions to ask and where to find answers.

Sun Tzu says it is important to appraise an impending battle through five fundamental factors—politics; climate; terrain; commander; doctrine and vision. This still holds true. Don't make any strategic decisions until these five factors are known. Once the appraisal is made, the leader can then compare various scenarios between the two sides to figure what the results of a war might be. Only then can the leader decide whether to stand back or join the battle and win the war. Here are the five factors, adapted for modern businesses, and why they're important.

1. Politics. Including government rules, internal company politics, and technology prejudice among both your customers and your employees. It also includes understanding the leadership and politics of archrivals who might become your allies at a moment's notice. When Vivendi, a French water utility that branched into telecommunications and Internet services in the late 1990s, made its 2000 bid for Seagram, an entertainment and spirits company, it looked like an ultimate clash of cultures. Leadership and employees were from different countries and spoke different languages. But the differences ran even deeper. Though a publicly traded company, Seagram was still a family operation at heart, like Ford Motor Company has been for years. Samuel Bronfman founded the forerunner to Seagram in 1924; Edgar M. Bronfman was chairman at the time of the Vivendi merger. Vivendi, however, was an aggressive growth, investor-driven company.

Their views on which entertainment spaces to target differed, too. Seagram was Hollywood-oriented, through its ownership of Universal Studios. Vivendi was interested in print publishing and online content, viewing that as the future of multimedia. Only the test of time can prove how this clash of cultures will play out. The combined company could enjoy many synergies, if it can overcome its potential political land mines. Luckily, both sides seem committed to deal with the differences and find common ground through the creation of Vivendi Universal.

2. Climate. In classic battle situations, this comprises the weather and the overall environmental factors of the city or countryside where a battle will take place. If you attack, will your troops become mired in snow? Overcome by heat? Dizzy from lack of air at high elevations? But on the Internet, this factor means your business climate plus the business climate in which your opponent operates. This also includes the status of the current economy and the mood of customers, as well as internal factors. Are you a shirt-and-tie operation like IBM used to be, or are you a shorts-and-T-shirts company with a Ping-Pong table in your lobby? Does your opponent have a huge marketing budget that can plant its company logo and a smiling face at every major trade show?

Climate can also mean the state of the Internet—the existing and emerging online technologies, and the public's willingness to accept certain changes. Online trading centers created by companies such as Datek and Ameritrade are prime examples of tools, and even full businesses, that evolved as the competitive climate changed toward online self-directed investing. As more people used the Web to collect business information and analyze their personal finances in the late 1990s, the opportunity arose for trading as they read news and stock charts. This happened as the general public became more at ease with finding business news and making financial transactions online. Business developers who correctly read that climate change became the first movers to win this new market. This forecasting ability allowed companies like E-Trade and Datek to quickly steal business from monolithic investment firms that once totally controlled their industry. The newcomers gained distribution for their services via icons on investment news sites. These links took customers directly to the new stock-trading tools they could use.

3. Terrain. In the classic sense, this factor asks, Are you going to do battle from high ground or low? In a swamp? Far away, or near home? In Internet terms, it asks, Do you have the connectivity you need? The bandwidth? The machines? Will you own or lease machines, software, and office space? Will you outsource minor functions or entire departments? Are you operating mostly in Windows, Unix, Mac, Mainframe, or some custom-built flavor? In modern business, terrain comprises the wires, gigabytes, and mindshare of your customers.

If you're an established company, you may have a full-scale business process already in place, and you may have already moved your existing Oracle database and order-entry forms online using special Oracle Web tools. If you're a start-up, perhaps you prefer to build a rapid prototype of your information flow, using something like Allaire's Cold Fusion to construct a quick online catalog of products, and build the associated order forms virtually overnight. Your approach depends on your current terrain and position.

Other terrain issues include the speed of the Internet connections at your offices and at the homes or offices of your customers. What technologies or products do your business partners use, and are you compatible with them? What technologies do your opponents use? Your customers? Your opponent's customers? If you don't know all the complexities of your playing field, you are not properly oriented for the contest. Understand this terrain before making business decisions with far-reaching consequences. Remember the original Boo.com's decision to spend millions building a stunning shopping site with sharp colors and rotating 3-D product pictures. Their efforts resulted in an enormous visitor dropout rate because pages loaded slowly and many customers didn't have the plug-in software necessary to view the 3-D images. The original idea was to target Web-savvy customers, so Boo assumed speed and plug-ins weren't an issue. But they misjudged the terrain. The original effort ended in bankruptcy, and the site was shuttered. The name was sold, and the site now lives on with a much more plausible design.

4. Commander. Is the leadership of your company and your opponent's company Internet savvy and equipped for key roles, like forming alliances? Does the leader understand the new economy and the Net-based marketplace? Will the CEO receive support from stockholders and the board of directors if major organizational changes are needed to compete on the Internet? Cahners Business Information, then called Cahners Publishing, moved aggressively into the Internet in 1996. The Net seemed a perfect match for this organization that specializes in quality business magazines distributed free to qualified readers. Cahners had a leg up on other publishers who were nervous about offering content for free on the Web. Since Cahners already gives away its content and makes its money from highly targeted advertising, why wouldn't the Web be an obvious extension? But infighting about how the new online versions of the magazines should be structured compared to the print versions caused friction amongst publishers of the individual titles, which led to development delays and revenue-sharing issues. Some projects were started, then abandoned as publishers claimed to own certain turf within the company.

The initial investment was made to establish Web versions of several of its industrial magazines, but Cahners management delayed investing in newer technologies such as dynamic content delivery and active server pages. They ended up with a very maintenance-heavy site, and leaner operations like VerticalNet began to ramp up and steal some of their business through competing sites that were easier to build and maintain.

Perhaps Cahners' biggest blunder was its hesitancy to move from a pure subscription model to a free (or at least cheaper) Web-based model for its crown jewel, the massive Lexis-Nexis online archive of news articles and legal information. Managers resisted allowing free access because the traditional subscription model generated lucrative returns. They initially resisted setting Lexis-Nexis up as a provider of news feeds to subscriber media sites. This foot-dragging through 1999 created opportunity for companies like Brint.com and Internet Wire to gain a foothold in this market. Other competitors like Comtex, iSyndicate, and ScreamingMedia sprang up to provide news-content feeds to small- to medium-sized Web sites. These smaller companies' activities posed a serious challenge to Cahners, who might have been the reigning king in content-feed space for vertical industries had leaders moved more aggressively at the onset.

As you appraise the leadership of your organization and your opponent's, ask yourself, Does the leader understand the new currencies afoot, and that an exchange rate for traditional currency must be established before transitioning to the new economy? Does your CEO or business development staff realize when to give or take an equity stake in another company instead of cash, or trade your own equity for eyeballs that will see your product or service? Does your board of directors have a mind of its own, or is the board a rubber stamp for CEO decisions? Do leaders know which markets are growing and which are shrinking, and can they develop appropriate products for these markets? Are the leaders players? Or do they mostly play catch-up?

5. Doctrine and Vision. This is the organization and belief system of the group. It's the structure of the organization and its system of accountability so that work actually gets done. It's about the discipline to make things happen, and not blaming others for failures. It's also a sense of buy-in from those who must do the work to keep things on track and an understanding, throughout the ranks, of the logistics needed to make any process happen. It's building a real team, not a group of individuals biding time and polishing their resumes. Builders of personal empires sometimes have a tough time working within an Internet-savvy organization, even if they are brilliant MBAs with superior knowledge of specific markets. The Net is all about breaking down walls, sharing information, and multitasking.

Vision is about keeping one's eye on the ball. But more than that, it's a company-wide standard, almost a code of ethics, that says teammates will not let each other down, and they will not build second-class products. Few companies work from a doctrine and a vision that they use to make this type of commitment. Those that do, succeed.

In its early days, Apple Computer had such a doctrine. Its commitment to build "insanely great" products was evident from leader Steve Jobs, who would scream when prototypes failed to meet expectations. It was evident in engineers who worked all night to build graphical interfaces that blew away the competition. It even gave rise to the concept of a product evangelist, in the days when Guy Kawasaki would traverse the tech world to convince others to participate in technology development for the Macintosh. But the doctrine seemed lost by the mid-1990s when Apple diverged into too many projects and lost not only market share but a perceptible path for remaining creative and profitable. Apple finally regained its original sense of uniqueness and electricity when Jobs returned to the helm after several years, but its struggle continues.

Those who master the facts and nuances of these five factors own the knowledge to win. But this does not mean that a person or organization with the clear advantage in any one of these categories will automatically be the winner. It's a matter of honest appraisal and educated decisions based on whatever advantages or disadvantages you perceive. Timing and industry acceptance of your efforts are paramount.

KPMG International working with Benchmarking Partners recently defined four types of e-commerce companies. Where does your company fall on this scale?

- **Players** are those who are active in e-commerce and consider e-commerce projects to be highly important. Chemical, consumer goods, and retail industries are often players. Mostly, the top players are companies whose products are considered commodities. They're forced to use the Net to gain every possible advantage, to shave points off their costs and improve their supply chain.
- **Planners** are companies who will increase e-commerce activities in the future. Some of their projects are already in the e-commerce

planning stages. Transportation and third-party logistics providers (people who handle product logistics issues between two other companies) fall into this category. Ironically, although the transportation industry practically invented online tracking of inventories and orders, many in this industry are still in the planning stage. Perhaps the reason is because the most difficult piece is to develop full end-to-end systems that include every aspect of a purchase, right down to its delivery.

- **Planters** are those who give e-commerce a low priority rating, but who have some initiatives underway. They don't necessarily recognize the strategic importance of e-commerce, but they're investigating it because they feel they should. Some wholesale and retail operations are planters. Local stores with a solid customer base don't see a reason to migrate to Internet sales anytime soon. Local furniture or music stores probably have Web sites and vague ideas that they'll sell things through that Web site eventually, but business isn't bad so, hey, what's the hurry?

- **Plodders** are companies with both low e-commerce activity levels and low importance ratings for online transactions. Utilities and old-style industrial products companies tend to be plodders. Your local convenience store is a plodder. A large canning factory or a piano manufacturer are probably plodders. The reason isn't that they lack a competitive nature, it's that online sales are not a major attraction for these businesses. A convenience store is in business because it's convenient. You're not going to order a cup of coffee online from a convenience store and wait two days for delivery. A canning factory that worked with the same suppliers and distributors for years doesn't need to branch out quickly. And who's going to buy a piano online? The manufacturer may offer an online catalog with nice pictures of its products, and it may take a trickle of orders via the Net. But most people want to play a piano, feel its keys, and listen to it before purchasing.

Sometimes plodders are very happy being plodders, and they'll remain prosperous even if they don't change. But if you're a plodder who should strive to change because your business could benefit from online sales, it's best to make an aggressive move into Internet marketing and sales. It's also important to make sure your e-commerce strategy solidly matches your overall corporate strategy, with long-term plans in place. Another study conducted by Benchmarking Partners found that most companies who moved into e-commerce did so for specific and limited applications without a strategic e-commerce initiative. They lacked a centralized e-commerce director, they could not list company-wide e-commerce spending, and they could not assure that various e-commerce platforms within the company were compatible and capable of sharing crucial data. Without such knowledge, you are a plodder, even if you don't intend to be.

Hard Questions to Ask about Yourself in Relation to *Them*

Answering the following questions will help you build a knowledge base and dig deeper into where you stand on the five factors previously outlined.

1. Leadership
   - Which CEO or president is more talented, cunning, and hardworking? Who can best establish a vision and motivate employees?
   - Who on the board of directors is more wise, able, and experienced? If you are competing with a small private company that lacks a board, ask these same questions about the major investors and advisors.

2. Positioning
   - Which company has, or is likely to obtain, a distinct advantage in business climate or operating terrain? Who has the best working situation, the best hardware and software, and the best resident skill set? Would you rather work with them or compete with them?
   - Is the company's business plan and corporate life-cycle plan short-term (develop a technology and market advantage, then be acquired) or long-term (be a viable, growing business with plans to stand alone as long as necessary)? Neither is the wrong approach. Knowing what their plan is can help you make the right strategic decisions.
   - Who operates from the most attractive location that appeals to the best workers and offers the best lifestyle?
   - Who can pay more or offer the premium stock-option package?
   - Is there a heavy reliance on contractors and temporary workers? That can be good in some circumstances and bad in others, depending on the company's long-term prospects and expenses, and how it operates from contract to contract.
   - Is your company built to last, or built to flip? In other words, do you want to have a long-term presence, or do you want to be acquired? What about your competitor? What about the partners who help your company succeed? How could the flipping of other companies affect you?

3. Skill and discipline
   - In which organization are the instructions of management best implemented? In which organization are the processes of product development most efficiently executed?
   - Which company's workers are more educated, talented, and hardworking? Note: Compensation can be a big factor here. Judge carefully—in some cases workers are overeducated and ill-suited for their jobs.

- What is the employee turnover rate? Low is good as long as the company isn't stodgy. High is not necessarily bad if new, talented workers are acquired in a steady stream and salary costs are reduced.
- Are there ongoing training and educational development opportunities for all workers? If not, is that something you offer that could draw employees away from a competitor?
- Which company administers rewards and punishments in a more enlightened and correct way? For example, are salary increases and stock options based on performance? How are unproductive workers reassigned or handled? How are layoffs conducted? Are significant bonuses awarded for products that are delivered beyond spec, ahead of time, and under budget?

If you can answer these questions honestly and correctly, you can attain a complete picture of the competitive landscape, which is essen-

QUICK TRICKS

Download a searchable copy of the VARBusiness 500 listings from www.varbusiness.com. It's a listing of the top value-added resellers, integrators, and IT consultants in business today. As a starting point to grow your business, it identifies key competitors and starts your competitive analysis, possibly helping you identify partnership possibilities. The investment is $300, which is much less than you'd pay one of your employees to gather this information on company time. Visit places like CNet (www.cnet.com), Internet World (www.internet.com), Computer Select (www.computer-select.com), Quote.com, Lexis-Nexis (www.lexis-nexis .com), or Standard & Poor's (www.standardandpoor.com/). Each site, competing head-to-head on the Internet for *your* business, holds a wealth of information about you and your competition.

tial for any battle. You can predict who is likely to gain or lose market share. Go to trade shows. Read trade magazines. Pore over full-blown analyst reports. Talk to ex-employees of your competition. The information is out there. Collect it. Discover what works for others and absorb their process and technology, then leverage it with your own special flavor.

Not So Covert Operations—A Case Study in the Power of Analysis

In later chapters that prepare you for battle, you learn how spy operations can benefit your company. IBM was known to do fantastically detailed competitive analyses on Sun Microsystems and Hewlett-Packard. The level of specifics is astounding but provides a good blueprint for how thoroughly you should understand your competition today. One IBM report details Sun's influence in seven market segments—enterprise resource planning for large companies, supply chain management, front-office systems, data warehousing, design automation and engineering, software development, and e-commerce. The report continues by showing Sun's influence spread across five industry segments—retail, energy, healthcare, publishing, and service providing. It drills all the way down to detailed percentages of business in certain sectors and then for specific accounts in which it believes Sun has focused extra energy.

The report goes on to discuss Sun's foray into advanced disk arrays for data-storage systems, and predicts Sun will initially try to capture the storage associated with Sun's own server sales, then branch out from there. (Many companies have matched other manufacturers' storage systems with their Sun servers for big applications, so this is a logical place for Sun to steal back some business.)

The detailed IBM reports are a classic example of one competitor knowing the exact strengths and weaknesses of another competitor, complete with a prediction of how marketing muscle and developmental limits will prompt the competitor to its next step.

Great to have, but how should one actually use such elaborate knowledge?

One use is to know when and where a competitor will be ready for a fight, and to know where they feel vulnerable and likely to avoid a fight. IBM leaders can read these reports and decide if they should challenge Sun's strategy of selling storage units to current customers, or allow Sun to focus on that specific market segment while IBM concentrates on a different segment.

This is a good time to introduce one other key point that many great leaders know: **One of the best ways to win a battle is to make your opponent choose not to fight.** They will not fight you if they believe they will lose. When Microsoft Corporation reached its zenith, you didn't see many other companies stepping forward with a new word processor or spreadsheet product. Microsoft Word and Microsoft Excel were the acknowledged kings in this arena. End of story. Few dared challenge them.

That's the easiest battle to win—the one that the enemy avoids.

Surprisingly, where a Microsoft challenger did appear was to the Microsoft Windows operating system. But why would anyone tackle the firmly entrenched, dominant OS?

The challenger dared to make its claim by initially focusing on a different, albeit smaller, market space and business model. The upstart Linux operating system was aimed at users who preferred Unix and who wanted to run Unix on Intel-chip PCs. In this case, Linux did not establish a new market space per se. It attacked a tiny fraction of a huge market and focused on people who wanted free software. It gained a foothold with some loyal followers before it ever appeared on the radar as a threat.

The distribution model for Linux was far different from Microsoft's, even downright radical. Linux is distributed as free software. Because Linux didn't directly challenge Microsoft, but rather a small segment of the overall OS market, it was able to continue building on that foothold. It then grew to the point where it became a true challenger, slowly intruding into Microsoft's turf at a vulnerable time when the giant was busy with a massive federal investigation.

> **Find and take over a space where your opponent has no allies. Grab a position that your opponent isn't sure is worth fighting for. Work when your opponent is distracted elsewhere. Pick a vulnerable time.**

Analyzing Linux in recent years, it also was difficult to predict that this upstart with no clear leader at the helm would someday rise to challenge Microsoft as a dominant OS. Linus Torvalds may have started Linux, but its open model, allowing anyone to offer additions and modifications, makes Linux effectively leaderless. Linux hasn't won yet. It likely will not win in the classic sense of total market domination. But it survives and prospers because it owns its space, shows no fear, and sets the rules for battle.

use the internet: your weapon to wage business war

the e-world loves to endlessly debate about what the Internet is, and what it is not. Certainly, no single enterprise can really quantify the total reach of this network of networks that intersects so many different operations and affects so many business processes. No single person could ever visit and interact with all the different parts and technologies that make up the Net, nor incorporate all these possibilities into one business.

Trying to specify what the Internet *is not* also sparks debate. **Internet technologies are chameleon-like, and can be molded into whatever you want,** as long as you're willing to commit enough development dollars and marketing muscle into development. Do you want the Internet to be a digital version of network television? Do you want it to be a bank? A retail store? A marketing and commerce platform for a Fortune 500 company? A three-dimensional space you can enter and walk around inside? It can be all this and more. The question for you is how to transform your interaction with the Net into whatever you need it to be to extend your business.

What the Internet can become is limited only by the amount of information that can be shoved down the pipe at any one time. Unfortunately, that's a very real limit. We won't have Star Trek–like Holodecks, or even a decent 3-D shopping area where you can pick up and examine products, for quite some time. (That's what Boo.com tried and failed miserably.) What we do have are remarkable nascent efforts like reverse auctions, personalized procurement portals, and the multifarious name-your-own-price philosophy of priceline.com, which prove that what is being built today is not business as usual.

The Internet merges or extends so many different concepts and methods of business that it's fair to say it's not a revolution at all. Instead, the Internet is a moderate evolution in communications that looks massive in scale because everything is evolving at once.

When every retailer, every media outlet, every manufacturing process, every logistics system, and every entertainment company restructures their processes simultaneously, using the same technical underpinnings, the world is bound to notice. It's like the old joke that says the world would wobble if everyone in China climbed onto their chairs and jumped off together. Our world has been shaken simply because many different types of businesses discovered the Net at the same time and jumped on it.

Surprisingly, even executives of important Net services share this view. "I'm not one of those people who thinks the Net changes everything," said VerticalNet chairman Mark Walsh. "I think everything changes the Net. Of course, what it also does is accelerate the speed by which bad companies are punished and good companies are discovered and rewarded."

Fundamentally, the Net has not changed basic business practices. Rather, the reverse is happening. **The Net is morphing to adopt basic business practices including specific types of accounting and order processing.**

What has truly changed is the way the data flows between organizations. What the rise of the Internet has forced are changes on the consumer side.

For example, "We all found that the stereo we saw on the shelf for $220 could be bought online for $190. We changed our buying habits," said Walsh.

Where business had to adapt was in the migration of customers to new ways of locating and purchasing products. But the migration toward cheaper goods has not been universal. For manufacturers, the issue isn't always price. More often, it's about reliable product supply, dependable service, and consistency of offerings. That's why the terms B2B (business to business) and B2C (business to consumer) became such buzzwords at the turn of this century. They identify increasingly different markets with increasingly different needs.

But this chapter isn't about cheerleading how wonderful the Internet is, nor is it meant to spotlight new online markets. It's about how current and future Net technologies can be used to wage business warfare. Understanding what the Internet is, and what it can be, is just the starting point. Your first challenge is to deal with all those people who view the Internet as just another battlefield to be conquered.

Understand the breadth of what the Net is, and you'll realize it's much more—much different—than strictly a battlefield.

Wise businesspersons who want to compete will stop focusing on an isolated Internet strategy and start integrating Internet activities into all parts of their business plans, from accounting, to marketing, to distribution of products or content. They will stop thinking of the Net as an outside force to be defeated, and start thinking of it as the road they must travel to satisfy their needs and deliver their products.

These multiple facets illuminate many competitive niches to be exploited. Companies that want to leverage e-commerce opportunities need to understand these manifold components. "I wouldn't want the

LOOK AT THE INTERNET AS ALL THESE THINGS:

- a weapon, because it can be used to share development tasks with partners and for building applications to deliver your products and services;

- a communications system, for sharing information internally and externally, and for delivering your marketing message;

- a logistics service that can track goods, predict needs, and route materials ahead of your needs;

- a reconnaissance vehicle that provides you with competitive research and detailed business data;

- an automated business process that applies a set of rules to channel information through your system.

word e-commerce to get confused with 'We sell stuff,' " said Matt Comyns, CNET vice president of business development. "In our case, we've been able to create great branding without actually selling stuff. We hit a sweet spot." For CNET, that translates to helping people find information on computers, plus a way for buyers and sellers to find each other.

VerticalNet's Walsh echoes the concept that the Net in isolation is not a unique niche for your business to win. "There are people who think the Internet itself is some new battleground, or it's Darwin's theory in action, but it's not," Walsh told me in a phone conversation. "I tell them to think of the Internet as a digital sales channel, nothing more, nothing less. It's not some tectonic shift."

Both Walsh and Comyns acknowledge that sales and communications aspects of the Net boost competition to new levels. But the competition is still in the marketplace, where it's always been. The Net is the catalyst that's lit huge fires across those marketplaces. "The challenge to big companies is that they are often protected by big margins," Walsh said. "They're protected by their sales channels and profit centers, and these things give them a certain power. They're on the back pages of the trade magazines and they have the biggest booths at the trade shows. But those margins will come under duress by savvy consumers who are empowered by information. Buyers can find better sales channels now by using better online directories and communities."

E-commerce sites that help build industry-specific communities, like VerticalNet, Vignette Corporation, Ariba, and I2 Technologies' TradeMatrix, have extended and reshaped the logistics of marketplace competition. They've effectively taken the wind out of the sails of big companies who had been riding their big profit margins to success via sheer momentum. **Get to know the communities within your industry and learn what they can do for you. Participate in community-building efforts to find new commerce opportunities and ways to trim your margins.**

This doesn't mean we're heading into an era with no dominant players in key industries. In his book *The Gorilla Game*, Geoffrey Moore aptly describes how modern markets adopt certain technologies and attitudes that push a single company into an enduring leadership position for each market segment. He terms this concept the technology adoption life cycle and refers to the leading companies in each business niche as a gorilla—a tough force to reckon with and even tougher to displace. The concept is particularly suited for high-tech, product-oriented companies that sell into mass markets undergoing big growth spurts—because you can see the evolution happen quickly.

As a market matures, you either must be a gorilla or serve the gorilla in your market niche. The ultimate example is Microsoft. No one is going to displace this 8 million pound gorilla from its dominant position anytime soon (broken up or not). Yet many fortunes have been made by smaller companies that partner with or feed into the Microsoft leviathan. Likewise, Cisco is the dominant player in the network hardware niche. Companies that supply Cisco, such as Hifn, which provides security processors for Cisco's broadband routers, perform very well by serving the gorilla in their market.

Before you can effectively use the tools of online commerce, you have to decide not only what your company's core competency is (you can have more than one focus, as long as you have the resources to sustain them all), you must also know if you are, or can be, the dominant player. At a certain point, you may have to accept that someone else is the central player, and adjust your business model accordingly. The mistake many make as they venture into e-commerce and Web development is that they don't know on what to focus. They have a vague notion that page views are an important measure. They know that money is made from transactions. But unless you're looking to compete with the large portal sites, raw page views may be the wrong focus.

Traffic, community building, and revenue streams come in many forms. For example, there are many products in a supermarket, yet the farmers and factories that produce the products seldom own a supermarket. Nor do they own the cash register or the computers that track inventory for the supermarket. They aren't in that business. Any business building an e-commerce presence needs to decide if they want to be a market maker, the provider of the content that attracts the people to the market, the entrepreneur that interacts with market makers as they congregate, or the occupant of one of a thousand other available niches.

It may be that only the market maker need worry about raw page views. Others need to worry about the quality of those pages, and the income they produce. Meanwhile, advances like streaming media, instant messaging, and Web-enabled cell phones may supersede page views as a central focus in the months ahead.

Outside of page views and time to market, management of quality as well as people and facilities remains important for a growing organization. So is attention to detail. In fact, details become extremely important in a large organization because processes get increasingly lost if they are ignored. Information isn't shared. Balls are dropped.

Things are built incorrectly, and unlike a small team, the people who might notice a problem aren't working closely enough to notice the missing details and fix them. They may work in a different building and never notice problems until it's too late.

The New Market Cycle

Let's focus for a moment on one facet of the Internet—the Net as a market space. Many .com companies mobilized in the late 1990s to take over market share via an online presence. These included many types of businesses, from media companies to Web-site hosting to e-commerce exchanges. A pullback in stock prices ensued in spring 2000, followed by a shakeout of the most speculative companies for the rest of that year. Watching this happen was a key lesson in how any market typically evolves. In many ways, it's no different than what happens when any new frontier opens, including events like the Oklahoma land rush in 1889.

New markets evolve through this series of phases. Whatever your market space, it's important to assess the phase it is in, and how that affects your business prospects. Not knowing this basic orientation is akin to entering battle without knowing who you are fighting, where the front lines are, and what you're trying to win.

1. The land grab occurs to stake out a position in the new terrain/market.

2. Adapt as you travel further along the new terrain. Rapid innovations serve different portions of the market and the market's new needs.

3. Speculative investment is awarded to promising new businesses and new technologies as they gain a foothold. A market bubble forms as the rising tide raises all boats, since it's not yet clear who the winners will be. In this stage, a profit-to-earnings ratio (P/E) is far less important than the growth potential of a company.

4. Key players are recognized and rewarded with both increased sales and market share.

5. The bubble bursts and some businesses fail. These include poorly managed companies, late arrivals, and even some promising companies with good solutions who are unfortunately unnoticed in the noisy marketplace. Likewise, those who supply the new business with goods and services are also affected by these failures because there are now fewer companies to sell to.

6. The market consolidates into a handful of key players. At this point, profits become much more important for the survivors, though growth potential remains significant to a company's stock price.

7. Everyone in the market learns from the rise and fall and the failures and successes of other players. The market matures and growth returns, though not at the wild initial pace.

8. Innovation leads to new niches and potential new markets, and the process begins again, most likely on a much smaller scale than what occurred for the Internet.

Today, the Internet as an evolving market is hovering around step five of this process. Top online portal companies like Yahoo, AOL, and Lycos are being recognized and rewarded, even though their stock prices take occasional hits. Top online retailers like Amazon and Egghead are struggling but maintaining a foothold. Top supply chain and vertical community aggregators like VerticalNet and Open Market are gaining notice and big-buck participants, but remain threatened by competing community-building centers. The list goes on, but wild speculation in these pioneering companies has drawn to a close. The initial bubble burst and the shakeout is well underway, though speculation continues in fringe technologies. This is a highly competitive time, and only those with a solid business plan, an eye on profits, and the ability to accurately read and react to the market will survive.

One thing the market demands at the moment is better target marketing and product relevancy. Service personalization is a recurrent theme for any business broadening its online reach. Focus your expenditures on creating tools for customer personalization, and your investment should pay off in the long term.

Know Your Constituencies

A paper from the research firm Jupiter Communications titled *Proactive Personalization: Learning to Swim, Not Drown in Consumer Data,* discusses the relevance of the Net in getting closer to customers. "Jupiter contends that personalization is evolving into a core element of site infrastructure," it adds, "as Web ventures make a transition from ad hoc implementations to building the necessary infrastructure to manage and integrate consumer data. The next phase in personalization involves the use of appropriate analytical tools to draw value from these data and drive a consistent targeted message across site applications."

Personalization should be viewed as an ongoing, ever-expanding process rather than a discrete technology that can be purchased or controlled. It is a key piece of ammunition as you compete to serve your marketplace. Rather than seeking out and purchasing personalization companies or tools, most Net companies invest in building a flexible information management infrastructure to accommodate a range of data sources, data drilling, and display techniques that are unique to their customers.

There's a Web site and consulting service called Personalization .com, underwritten by Net Perceptions (but evidently open to competitors) that provides advice and solutions for businesses that want to build and utilize evolving client profiles to channel customized information and opportunities to their clientele. **The goal is to deliver value to those customers, gaining customer loyalty and, to a certain extent, dependence.**

Meanwhile, Microsoft's MSN Explorer, introduced in September 2000, built personalization directly into the browser, extending the concept to something that's carried with the surfer at all times. Clearly, personalization has been, and continues to be, an important tool in many businesses' online arsenals. Those seeking to expand their online reach should not ignore the trend.

The Cost of Waging War

The cost of waging an all-out war to control an Internet market space is phenomenally expensive, especially if your goal is to offer e-commerce services and online ordering. Those who are only beginning to explore online markets may be surprised at the cost of developing an e-commerce–enabled site. They may spend anywhere from a few thousand dollars—to develop a basic online catalog, hosting it at a limited Web merchant provider like FreeMerchant.com—to millions of dollars for a full-service system with real-time inventory management and integration into their accounting and enterprise resource management systems.

A recent Gartner-Group survey asked 100 leading companies operating sales sites how much money they spent on e-commerce system development, and the average was $750,000 for basic technology and labor. Add to that the cost of developing accounting and order fulfillment systems, plus the cost of marketing and advertising. Some sites easily broke the $10 million mark.

Yet such development can be faster and cheaper than waging a traditional business war. **Remember that the Internet sharply compresses time and space. It can also compress development costs.** Imagine the money a large retailer might spend in a traditional retail venture, scouting property for a new store, then ramping up local operations, staffing, advertising, shipping, inventory, and so on. Think of the associated costs for necessities like shelving and display, lighting, decorating, and shopping carts. The same $10 million could easily be spent expanding a traditional business, too, and signs of success or failure would take much longer to surface.

In the manufacturing industry, the mantra has long been "better, faster, cheaper" and engineers and accountants constantly strive to improve a product, cut costs, and remain competitive. Online ventures have a slightly different question to ask. (And it's not, "Wouldn't 'Better, Faster, Cheaper' be a great name for a rock group?") They ask how they can develop a working system *fast* and *cheap* to gain first-mover status for their new venture. They'll work on the better part of the equation a few months later.

For a Net-based venture, react quickly, develop your prototypes quickly (using rapid application development tools), and then discover, rather quickly, if your concept looks successful and if your development should continue. This is done via both in-house and real-world testing. It is a stressful, high-risk environment. But there is less risk of throwing good money after bad because you can quickly realize if you are on the right path before you invest years of work and multimillions of dollars in development money.

For example, Autobytel.com, one of the largest, most comprehensive automobile shopping sites on the Internet, faced a dilemma in 1996. Its original site was designed using straight HTML pages and Perl scripts, and it was hosted on machines leased from an Internet service provider. Managers decided to bring the site in-house as they developed a new system that could scale to millions of users. The effort to revamp everything began in late fall. The new site was in place by January, and able to handle those millions of visitors in the few days following Autobytel's ad during the 1997 Superbowl.

To accomplish this, the company chose Allaire's Cold Fusion, which provides a Web application server with an integrated development environment. The front-end Web server passes queries to the Cold Fusion server, which serves dynamic content generated via data feeds from several sources. These range from auto inventory lists from dealers (updated every day) to loan rates offered by multiple banks.

Compare this to a more traditional method of developing a business database back in the old days of the early 1990s. Because it was difficult back then to add a new field or new functionality once a database was built, much more time was spent up front, studying needs and determining what fields to include. After the database was built, customized forms to query the database had to be built, often using proprietary tools provided by the database company. Data updates were performed at specific times, often in the middle of the night, and commonly the system went offline as the database was rebuilt.

With all these variables to consider, it's no wonder such efforts usually took months, and redesigns and enhancements occurred just once or twice per year. Rapid prototyping allows new ideas to evolve quickly and data configurations to change overnight.

Autobytel had a small lead on its competitors in 1996, and wanted to widen that lead by introducing new features as quickly as possible. That's why it switched to a rapid application development mode, according to an Allaire case study. And once its new system was built, it could deal with constantly updated data streams without shutting down its system for daily maintenance.

> Today, virtually no Web sites must go offline when databases are updated. Keeping up with the Joneses is very important if you want to compete.

But even with rapid development and real-time data feeds, the costs of resources (workers, machines, and physical space) and a good marketing campaign can accumulate to hundreds of millions of dollars. But you ramp up to this level. It's not what you'll spend right out of the starting gate, and that's a major break for new businesses.

A negative ramification of rapid application development is that there can be long-term complications when you don't spend as much time up front in the planning stage. Such applications are notoriously poorly documented because a programmer's or product manager's decision was made at 2 A.M. in order to build the system by morning. Then, as new functionality is needed, supplemental systems are constructed and hung off the original application in ways that would not be acceptable if all functionality had been considered and designed at the onset. What do you do when your development guru leaves? He or she may be the only one who truly knows how the system works.

> **All the risks related to your system may be acceptable if you're moving to capture market share. A better system can be designed and paid for later, after you've gained a few million dollars in new business.**

Established online businesses that are defending, rather than grabbing, new market share have a different focus. If you already control a major Internet market space, hundreds of millions of dollars is a reasonable expenditure to defend your business. If you're the newcomer, attacking and planning to seize control of an existing market space, you may have to spend even greater amounts to displace the current dominate player and maintain your momentum.

Some small companies become experts at partnering with other firms in order to form limited joint ventures to grow quickly. Others become whizzes at low-cost guerrilla marketing operations. Such companies are sometimes able to build business development and marketing momentum by operating outside the traditional channels, but expenses still rack up fast.

For example, CNET took a risk in the mid-1990s when it decided to capture a huge audience looking to download software. Comyns said the company studied CompuServe usage patterns during that era and discovered that one-third of people's time online was spent looking for and downloading software. This was an underserved market. CNET searched for a download resource and found it in Yugoslavia. A programmer there had created a spider that visited FTP sites and cataloged what was available. "We noticed this site on the Web and decided that he really nailed it," Comyns said. "The concept was that you really don't have to host all those files yourself. You can go out there and constantly search the free FTP sites and find the software you were looking for. That was our big foray into the downloads market." And it was the foundation for Shareware.com, still one of the most popular download sites on the Net. Buying the site and the technology from that Yugoslavian programmer was a great move for capturing a key market space.

The lesson on expense is clear. **There are ways to partner with others to reduce costs, but you still must commit to spending what is necessary to take over a market share and establish your beachhead for the years ahead.** Some traditional investors were baffled when the price of publicly traded .com companies were bid up to silly levels, such that even those .coms who made a profit had profit-to-earnings ratios that looked more like zip codes than workable quotients. Those who plowed nearly all profits back into the company for short-term gain won the battle during the land-grab phase. Savvy investors knew that those who were willing to spend and conquer had a better chance of being either a first mover or a key conqueror of prime market spaces.

Understand What You Are Asking of Your Employees

Sun Tzu says, "Those unable to understand the evils inherent in employing troops are equally unable to understand the advantageous ways of doing so."

As stated in the preface, Sun Tzu was not a man who admired war. As a general, he understood the evils and the hardship that come from war. Battle, no matter how small, is not to be taken lightly. It should be entered with a clear goal and an assertive battle plan, and it should be finished quickly. A well-timed and executed plan is the only way to assure victory, and it's the only way to assure expenses and losses will be minimized.

Marketplace battles and intense development projects also must be joined and finished quickly. This increases the chance of success because you quickly stake a claim and ultimately reduce the expenses and losses that accompany a protracted and unfocused effort.

Just as there are inherent evils in employing troops, there is a nastiness to grabbing market share or rolling out a new product that steals another company's business. Understand this pressure your employees experience, and help them achieve quick success.

Even protracted projects with long development times of a year or more must allow some ebb and flow of work and effort. The leader who understands this has a distinct advantage. Employees who know the deadlines, who can prepare for them, and who know they won't be constantly taxed with long work hours, except perhaps as deadlines approach, are more satisfied with their work.

Take advice from the battle master, but apply it to your unique needs as a businessperson who uses the Internet. Travel light. Plan well. Establish a rhythm for your work. Hit hard and fast, and finish the job quickly.

Sun Tzu also says, "Those adept in waging war do not require a second levy of conscripts, nor more than two provisionings to follow them into the field. They carry military equipment from the homeland, but rely on the enemy for provisions. Thus, the army is plentifully provided with food. They feed off the enemy."

A fast-paced corporation can operate the same way. There is nervousness about ramping up operations too fast. Where will you find qualified people? Where will you find the customers to pay off your extensive investment? But as you succeed, your success draws others into your sphere. You will become the winner that others invest in.

You will succeed the same way a conquering army uses the spoils of war to pay for its campaign. **In a military sense, the gold and plunder that is captured replenishes the gold that is spent to create and sustain the army.**

In business—in our more civilized but still competitive society—as you steal market share from your opponent, you also need their resources to sustain your growth. If and when your endeavors begin to succeed, you will take resources from your opponents, easing some of your organization's pressure. As you continue to succeed and grow, you will absorb the skilled employees who defect to your camp. If your success drives up the value of your company, you will be able to pick up market share and technologies through the purchase of other companies. You can integrate their engineers. You can finally absorb and build that skilled and knowledgeable sales force you've wanted.

At a certain point, you begin to rely on absorption for your expansion. It's a sign of success. And as you acquire larger organizations, you absorb a customer base along with everything else. It's one of the fastest ways to grow reach.

This is the developmental equivalent of an army that travels light. You drive your own costs up when carrying too many things along from the start, and not feeding off your opponent in small chunks.

As you create a new demand for resources in your area, prices of these resources rise. It's simple supply and demand. If you have the best engineers in a certain region, your opponent will have to increase what she pays to lure workers away from other regions of the country. Of course, you'll eventually have to pay more, too, but you'll have momentum on your side by then. When prices rise, the wealth of the other organization, especially an organization that lags in its product development, is drained away. When wealth is drained away, the other organization is afflicted with urgent problems that will distract and delay them.

You can impoverish your opponent by taking your battle to them. But you drive up your own costs, too. Instead, why not drive up the opponent's costs by making resources difficult to find? You may have to promise more to those whom you lure away, but your company's stock options are worth more because you're growing (that is, as long as you remain profitable).

Besides consuming employees, you can also capture the things that the opponent abandons or simply can't maintain, including services, outsourcing deals, specific technologies, advertisers, partnerships, and customers.

With this loss of wealth and exhaustion of strength, an organization becomes poor and disorganized. Its best human resources leave for better places. The organization switches from growth mode to maintenance mode, and eventually shrinks into survival mode, making do with the business it has, using its existing resources to stay alive rather than flourish.

This is the time when the company will be its most approachable if you want to purchase it. If it's an older company, perhaps its most valuable asset is its name, which may have wide recognition and a loyal customer base. How do you know if a company is open to acquisition?

"The obvious way is when they call you and ask if you'd like to buy them," said Walsh. "That actually happens a lot more than you'd expect. Second is when they start asking you about doing a strategic alliance."

Walsh said another indication is when the company's stock gets hammered downward. If you believe that its shareholders are financially savvy, you have to think they know something if a company's value starts declining.

When a general successfully feeds off the enemy, it drives up prices locally.

Sun Tzu says, "The country will be extremely poor and seven-tenths of their wealth dissipated. As to government expenditures, those due to broken-down chariots, worn-out horses, armor and helmets, bows and arrows, spears and shields, protective mantles, draft oxen, and wagons will amount to 60 percent of the total."

Sun Tzu also says a wise general not only ensures that his troops feed on the enemy, but he also realizes that every dollar of the enemy's provisions consumed equals 20 of one's own—basically because of the time and cost of logistics for moving provisions. Are his numbers accurate? It's unlikely that Sun Tzu ever attended a statistics or economics class, but his point is clear. You can bet your assets that captured enemy resources are worth more than yours, even if it's not a 20 to 1 ratio. Using the opponent's resources saves your own, it robs them of its supply, it heightens tensions within the other's camp, it helps you learn something of the opponent's processes, and it lets you protect and save your own resources for a later date.

But capturing resources from your opponent isn't easy. Your organization, your workers, everyone must be driven and eager to accomplish this. They must be courageous and believe in their leader in order to leap into a risky situation in which they must feed off the competition (chipping away their business and consuming their assets) in order to survive. If the leader doesn't follow through, capitalizing on even small bits of progress made by the employees, then that confidence is lost. A crisis of leadership ensues. Likewise, you can impoverish yourself with overly aggressive business tactics. There is a risk of overextending yourself as you find and train workers, buy technologies, and build a distribution system. The hit hard and finish fast lesson previously outlined will only take you so far.

A detailed business plan with real checkpoints and measurable cash flow is still as important as it was in traditional industries. When feeding off the enemy, you'll still find yourself in trouble if you bite off more than you can chew.

As you drive forward, conquering new markets, using the Internet to leverage alliances and feed off your opponent, you must never forget your staff. Without a doubt, after your initial business concept is structured and rolled out, your greatest follow-on opportunities are researched and eventually created by your workers. If you truly expect these workers to become courageous and hardworking enough to overcome your new opponents, they must be roused with both anger and reward.

Do you, as leader, have a system in place to reward the brave, the inventive, and the hardest working employees? Their attempts to earn you rewards are what will help you capture business of important strategic value.

> Sun Tzu says, "Therefore, in chariot fighting when more than 10 chariots are captured, reward those who take the first. Replace the enemy's flags and banners with your own, mix the captured chariots with yours, and mount them."

You can not afford to reward every member of your staff. Not everyone can be employee No. 1. If every staffer is rewarded, it cheapens the value of all rewards. It fails to spotlight those whose work is done well and done quickly. Instead, create a few truly valuable rewards and allow all staffers to compete for them. Today's rewards range from flextime to profit sharing.

> A chief goal for waging war is swift victory, not prolonged operations. The leader who understands this, and knows how to employ and reward workers to capture a specific market space effectively, satisfies his workforce and controls the fate of his company.

For example, within organizations that sell advertising on Web sites, there are often spiffs that are offered to promote a new sales opportunity. When a new section of the site rolls out, sales managers may offer a reward both for the first ad that's sold on the section, and for the greatest number of ads sold in that section. This helps sales-people keep the product in mind as they call their steady clients or work on new accounts.

Remember the Three Cs (and the Fourth C That Glues Them Together)

Sometimes, getting noticed isn't enough. Successful online ventures are those that achieve the magical mix hazily described as a community . . . and then leverage that community into a marketplace.

To make it all fit together, to build and maintain top-notch Web services, a site must aggregate three things:

1. **Content** is why the people come. Content can include news, catalogs, databases, special services, and message areas.

2. **Community** comprises the people who come for the content, to interact with other visitors and to buy things, either from the other visitors or the Web site itself. In many cases, people seek information for a business reason.

3. **Commerce** is what grows out of the community as people buy, sell, trade, or do research, based on the content they find and the ideas they share. Systems that add value to the process (i.e., by helping participants share business data or filter incoming information for business leads) command a higher price for their services and have a greater chance of building a bigger community from those who need such tools.

The fourth C in the mix is **context.** It's the ability to display content and commerce in a way that's logical for use by the community. Context is the toughest part of the mix for any Web venture. There are many sites with wonderful assets that fail to provide the proper navigation so visitors can find what they need. Others never find a good way to allow the community to connect and help each other, or never reach the critical mass necessary to spark a working community and marketplace.

In his book *Unleashing the Idea Virus* (available for free on the Net at www.ideavirus.com/), Seth Godin basically says that marketing by interrupting people isn't cost-effective anymore. "You can't afford to seek out people and send them unwanted marketing messages, in large groups, and hope that some will send you money." He says in the book's introduction, "Instead, the future belongs to marketers who establish a foundation and process where interested people can market to *each other*. Ignite consumer networks and then get out of the way and let them talk."

Online auction sites may be the best example of the three Cs placed in an optimal context. People can search for auction items, ask each other questions, view community opinions on sellers and buyers, view pictures, and basically interact in a way that keeps everyone interested. The content is created by the visitors, not paid staffers. And such sites become click farms that offer a mysterious mix of content and urgency that makes people return throughout the day to view page after page as they check their bid status.

Fulfilling all four Cs, including the commerce element, can be difficult and expensive. It's important to target your efforts and expenditures carefully. You not only need to create or purchase content for your community and develop applications they can use, you must spend money on proper site design and hosting, and on marketing efforts to drive the right users to your creation.

Those who have explored this know you must be willing to fund all these efforts going into the project. If you don't make the commitment to see the project through and provide the required funding, you're destined for failure, or at least a hard time and a lot of extra work as you try to play catch-up to make everything fall together.

Perhaps an implied fifth C looms large over any Web venture. That C is competition. If you're going to build something, take the job seriously and make the commitment to compete in a serious manner.

"If you play me in a game of table tennis, prepare for a death match," former Lycos CEO Bob Davis told a *Forbes* magazine reporter in the March 2000 issue. "I've had a relentless desire to win since my first [postcollege] job in sales. Ultimately, it's about winning and losing against the competition."

Such competition exists on every level in our society, from Fortune 500 companies to soccer moms who buy minivans, get up at 6 A.M., and spend hours on the sidelines, watching and cheering their competitive youngsters.

Someone, somewhere, has that competitive spirit, and wants to own the market space you occupy.

Firing Up to Face the Wide Landscape with Endless Mines

Waging war on the Net is expensive. Be well-funded or don't join the battle. Be ready to move in waves, because sustained full-bore efforts can drain employees.

Here's what Sun Tzu says about the expense of war.

"In operations of war—when one thousand fast, four-horse chariots; one thousand heavy chariots, and one thousand mail-clad soldiers are required; when provisions are transported for a thousand miles; when there are expenditures at home and at the front, and stipends for entertainment of envoys and advisers—the cost of materials such as glue and lacquer, and of chariots and armor will amount to one thousand pieces of gold a day.

"One hundred thousand troops may be dispatched only when this money is in hand. A speedy victory is the main object in war. If this is long in coming, weapons are blunted and morale depressed. If troops are attacking cities, their strength will be exhausted. When the army engages in protracted campaigns, the resources of the state will fall short."

Costs have gone up a bit since Sun Tzu's time. But the message still applies: You need to know your expenses before you execute your plan, and you need to commit enough money for the long haul so you don't fall short. It may be expensive to turn your Internet presence into your secret business weapon. But it's illogical to enter this battlefield with anything but the best weapon you can afford. An article titled "Sticker Shock" in the February 2001 issue of *Darwin* magazine predicted that most successful companies will earmark up to 25 percent of revenues for technology initiatives in the near future.

But the real lesson here is the need for speed. The longer your battle takes, the longer you hemorrhage money. While assembling a well-equipped army of the type Sun Tzu mentions is expensive, assembling a nimble, well-equipped army of developers, product managers, and marketing experts is equally expensive. Unlike traditional battles, your battle does not end when you win a market position. The battle to own that space continues. But the initial ramp-up and execution of the business is the opening salvo, and you must hit hard and follow through. You then control expenses for the long haul by committing the resources necessary to win this short-haul battle as quickly as possible.

After you've won the initial battle, it will take a different effort to maintain your position and protect the newly-won market by leveraging the Internet.

The tremendous intensity of your ramp-up phase can't be sustained.

Just as you may wait for others to look fatigued, others most certainly will look for signs of fatigue in your organization. Other companies will take advantage of any real or perceived crises of confidence. When they sense you are in disarray, they will seize market opportunities or lure away employees. Even a wise CEO will be unable to avert the disastrous consequences if others sense the time is right to move against you. There could be a wolf pack mentality, and your over-stressed organization could be the easy meat.

Sun Tzu's wave analogy is a good lesson. A working rhythm will wear down your opponent, and not you. A recent article in the Focus Magazine section of the Allbusiness.com Web site said that continually operating in crisis mode, plus high employee turnover rates, are signs that perhaps your business has grown too fast and has not established a proper rhythm for work.

The lesson is simple. The experts agree. Do not stay at high tide. Be like a wave. Establish a rhythm that lets you concentrate your efforts as needed, reaching higher and harder with each effort. It is the most efficient way to advance while assuring your workers that you have compassion for their needs and their human limits.

As you lap at the shore, carving out your successful niche, keep in mind that, in most markets, there will only be a few leaders. Can you become the Coke or Pepsi of your market? There are a fantastic number of Internet start-up companies each year, but few will become the dominant players in their spaces. Perhaps part of your strategy should be to anticipate which wave is the proper one to initiate your exit strategy. If you can't dominate, anticipate which project will be the one that gains you an edge in a particular area, which could make you a candidate for acquisition.

We have already seen at least one major Internet shakeout and consolidation. The NASDAQ market crash of April 2000 told the world that there were too many overvalued .com businesses. A shakeout helped clear out the minor players, dropping their silly market values down to something more manageable and understandable. The lesson is this:

We all know the process of elimination and consolidation that leads to the big few dominant players. We've seen it happen in the auto industry, the electrical power industry, and others. We're winding down to the big few portals that will be the access points and content distribution mechanisms, and the big few players in all other specialty areas, like investing, travel, entertainment, kids, and so on.

Online retailing may suffer the most brutal consolidation. A Forrester Research report from spring 2000, titled "The Demise of Dot

Com Retailers," said "Online merchants that smugly insist their brands and site design translate into financial assets will only fan the flames of investor scorn when profits don't materialize. These players won't secure the money they need to stay in business, as venture capitalists abandon retail in the search of the 'next big thing'—and redirect their money to emerging areas."

The study showed how the value of several major retailers had dropped over 80 percent from their peak market value in 1999. Value America, once a high flyer, dropped a whopping 96 percent between April 1999 and March 31, 2000. In August 2000, it filed for Chapter 11 bankruptcy protection. It made the move in order to drop its online retail business and restructure as an electronic services business.

Forrester said the ongoing collapse and consolidation of online retailers would result in displaced staffers heading off in two directions. "Executives born and bred in retail will return to the doorsteps of former employers—hat in hand—promising to inject Internet agility and innovation into their staid corporate cultures," the report said. "The question is, Will they bring any technical talent with them?" Meanwhile, programmers will likely head off to other marketplaces and IPO possibilities.

Of course, there will always be the vast "other" of the Net. The highly specialized sites that provide discreet services for special-needs clients. There will always be popular personal pages and new evolving technology sites. There will even be those fringe businesses that we use once and then forget, but which survive through a constant flux of new visitors. (How many U.S. parents ordered Japanese-language Pokemon cards directly from Japan during the height of that craze because their kids wanted something a bit different during their schoolyard card-swapping sessions?)

If you can be a specialist, like the coffee shop located in a train station, you don't have to worry about the big players or consolidation. You'll stay busy with new customers. But the big players already control the general-interest areas, from Yahoo to CNN. A new type of industry consolidation is looming, though, that can cloud the future.

Double Consolidation—The Unknown Factor

The other looming issue for .com, media, and telephone companies, is that it's not just the Internet marketplaces that are consolidating. **Products are consolidating, too, in a way that no industry has ever experienced.** At the same time we see the shake-up in .com companies, we also see computers merging with TVs, radios, and telephones; we see cell phones merging with pagers and Web browsers; and we see so-called computer media players merging into single interfaces that can play audio, video, and proprietary animations like MacroMedia's Flash.

At no time in history have such divergent products consolidated like this, blurring the lines between formerly stand-alone systems.

This makes consolidation on the business side very unpredictable. Let's say you've invested heavily in a company that presses and packages compact disks for music distributors. Let's say this company has a great business plan, and they've been very profitable and bought out their competitors. You feel wise and well-rewarded as they start to dominate their market. You invested in a gorilla. Except, suddenly PCs become stereos. Computer memory becomes music storage. The Internet becomes not only a broadcast medium, but also a way to find and order music. You have the best CD pressing factory in the world, and suddenly end users want to receive their music online via MP3 files.

Suddenly, you're like a buggy-whip maker because of double consolidation. This is the situation many high-tech competitors face today. They may have won the war on one consolidation front, but lost on another because they didn't see product technologies and preferences changing.

Luckily, this scenario hasn't happened yet. But as more people obtain high-bandwidth connections, can the CD industry continue to thrive? Or will it become another niche market?

It will always be wise to place your bets on a company rising to the top of its market space. Just watch closely for someone else who is figuring out a way to remove that whole market.

A complicating factor for .com companies is that there is not yet a single product that spans all associated industries. There is a general feeling that such a product will emerge, but it's not clear exactly what that will mean for each industry.

For now, we still have set-top boxes for our cable TV systems. We have PCs connected to phone lines or DSL modems, or maybe our cable systems. We have stand-alone radios in our cars and cell phones that offer, at the most, news headlines and stock quotes.

For now, streaming video viewed on a cell phone is laughable. Few people are now placing telephone calls through their PCs. And how many people actually surf the Web from their car dashboards? But very soon, we may do all these things, and we may do them from one appliance that's always with us. Therefore, both product and industry consolidation continues until this appliance is a reality. Will it grow out of the cell phone industry, the PC industry, the eyeglasses industry, or another industry entirely? That's an unknown right now. Be aware that even profitable companies with key technologies are at risk because they can be displaced by a surprise product consolidation.

This double whammy, merging markets and merging technologies, is what makes the Internet economy so unique. It's a war being fought on multiple fronts. In Sun Tzu's day, wise generals avoided fighting on many fronts. But in modern business, you don't have a choice. **At the very least, you need to monitor all technologies that peripherally touch your industry, so you'll have the necessary data to make strategic decisions.**

Access: The New Gold Standard

Pick up a piece of gold jewelry sometime, and think of what you're holding in your hand. That shiny piece of metal is the world's premiere example of the law of supply and demand. Gold is pretty. It's also resistant to tarnish and a good electrical conductor, which gives it many industrial uses.

People like it. Industry needs it. Yet if someone were to gather all the gold in the world and press it into a single cube, that cube could slide beneath the base of the Eiffel Tower with room to spare. That's the short formula for why gold is expensive. Great demand/limited supply = high cost.

Many have compared the Internet to a frontier gold-mining town where claims are staked and fortunes are made. But is it an accurate comparison? For one thing, gold-mining boom times had a central product—the gold itself—that created the boom. Is the Internet that sort of product? Or is it a market? Or maybe a service? Maybe it's simply a technology that's separate from all the applications it has spawned?

Those who argue that the Net is all the above may be missing something. There is indeed a single core service at the center of the Internet beanstalk. Without this driving force, none of its other parts would be possible.

Let's look at the parallel. Historically, when a new gold deposit is discovered (California, Alaska, and South Africa are the best examples), three types of people make money.

1. A few small operators work hard and get lucky, because they find at least a small amount of gold that makes the hard work worthwhile.

2. Large operators cast a wider net and know how to work smarter, conducting studies, buying specific tracts of land, and hiring (or exploiting) people to do extra work to reach a suspected deposit.

3. Some businesspeople provide goods and services to the miners and the boomtowns that grow up around them.

Gold was the pillar of the evolving frontier communities. It was the reason everything else sprang into being. Once the gold appeared, other markets, products, and services arrived and became deeply intertwined, to the point where a community evolved and in many cases survived even after the gold was gone. The communities included intertwined markets. There was a market for the people who bought the gold. There was a labor market. There was a market for land (whether it was claimed, purchased, or stolen). There was a market for transportation and logistics. Associated services included general stores, boarding houses, saloons, and in some cases, prostitutes. Associated products included clothing, equipment, and maybe beer or whiskey for those lonely Saturday nights when that's all a miner could afford.

So what is the similar driving force on the Internet? What is the core around which all other products and services evolve? **Endless debates have centered around whether the central product of the Net is a computing power, connections, the people who make up the Net, or the vast sea of databases connected to the Net. But it's none of these.**

The main pillar of the Net is simply this: ACCESS. This doesn't just mean access to the Internet itself. It means access to, well, everything in the universe.

Access to the Internet itself is the starting point. From there, people then find access to information, communities, markets, people, customers, ideas, solutions. Access to products is important, but it's the end game of a much larger process. That core concept of access is the central idea upon which all other Internet businesses exist.

The Internet started because people managing one computer needed access to data on another computer. The Net continues to grow in value every time another computer, person, or service plugs in because access continues to expand. All other Internet products hang from that central core called access.

To understand the market dynamics of the Net, it's important to realize how things have built out from this central idea. Years ago, when the first computers were plugged together to share data, someone was disintermediated, or removed from the process. That someone was the person who previously transferred data manually between machines (perhaps by reentering the data, or by carrying stacks of cards from one machine to the next).

This process of constantly improving access by disintermediating the go-betweens is the wedge that's driven the Internet ever deeper into the minds of consumers and businesses. People want access. Those who provide access are able to build a business around their service.

Companies that use the Web to find new business need to understand this progression. They may see their market share rise for a time as access to new customers is improved. But such businesses risk being disintermediated themselves if they don't understand the constant march the Net is making toward peer-to-peer access. Middlemen who improve access survive. Middlemen who are just middlemen can be bypassed.

understand internet time
and internet distance

Sometimes it seems the laws of physics that govern the online world differ greatly from the real world. Messages are exchanged instantly. A database across the country can be searched as quickly as a database down the hall. We move information instead of products, and somehow that makes the products cheaper. This makes people talk about Internet time like it's something removed from the physical world. **But we have to remember, in its wires and wavelengths, the Net obeys the same physical laws as we do. Time and distance just appear different when we view the world through a computer screen. We still need to extract reality out of its icons.**

When people say Internet time, what they're really talking about is the catalyst that the Net provides to speed up the regular workday. Internet time means working faster and more effectively. In Internet time, questions are usually answered in less than a day via e-mail (maybe faster in real-time chat). Product data is available instantly. Contracts are shuffled back and forth over the Net, with additions and changes highlighted in special colors. Work gets done quickly because of this catalyst. Without it, business lags and opportunities are lost.

Internet time has become the corporate standard today. It's tough to do business at a slower pace. VerticalNet's Walsh said that if he gets a business card from someone who doesn't have an e-mail address, he gives it back. "What's the point?" he laments. "It will be too hard to do business with them. A lot of our interaction would be through e-mail. Or when we are on the phone, I may ask them to go to a Web site with me. If you are not a connected person, then we aren't going to have a very robust relationship."

In fact, business needs now extend far beyond simple Net access. You can order full Net services at a click of a button, from hosted applications, to extra storage, to e-commerce systems that can instantly process credit-card transactions. Only a person accustomed to operating in Internet time is familiar with using such building blocks to ramp up a new business nearly overnight, working with new partners to put the various pieces of commerce, content, and accounting in place. "The new value proposition is how will you empower customers so that they can order and install Internet goods and services over the Net anytime they want, without having to talk to a salesperson," said Shawn Bice, an engineering director at Digex, a provider of high-performance Web- and application-hosting solutions. "They can implement and manage their e-business solution when they are ready to do it, through a browser."

This doesn't mean someone not used to working in Internet time cannot make such a leap. But it is likely that those who are used to working so quickly will pull away from those who don't.

Challenging Our Notion of Time

Not only are our ideas about the timeliness of communications changing, our concept of time itself, and how it should be measured, is changing. Time zones are an issue on the Internet because we can never be totally sure, across multiple zones, when a payment was received or an e-mail sent. And what time do chat meetings or digitally broadcast events really start? Since this is a worldwide network, it's never fair to claim that one part of the Net is ahead, or that someone's local time is the real time. (Even Greenwich time can't be considered the base time zone for the Net.) This problem has inspired several proposals on how Internet time should be measured. Netwide time solutions include proposals like swatch Internet time which divides the day into 1,000 swatches of 26.4 seconds duration. (Details are available at www.swatch.com.) There's also New Earth Time that takes a longitude-based approach, with each degree lasting four minutes as the earth turns, providing one universal Internet time. (Learn more at http://newearthtime.net/.)

It's far-fetched to think that these time solutions will catch on anytime soon. But the fact that they are needed indicates just how differently Internet time is perceived.

One thing is certain, the need for speed, and the need to participate at this new breakneck pace in order to remain competitive, has forever changed our concept of how business is done, and made us aware that Internet speed is indeed something transformed and wonderful.

When Distance Matters and When It Doesn't

Our concept of distance also has changed in obvious, and not-so-obvious ways. One obvious way is simple information access. It doesn't come from libraries anymore. The information you seek is probably not even on the bookshelves across your room. It comes from everywhere. You can reach everywhere from your desktop, and your desktop and your eyeballs can be reached from everywhere, by anyone.

Less obvious changes to our concept of distance include the way manufacturing and product distribution are handled. In years past, it was inappropriate to include such functions as part of the Internet. But manufacturing and distribution are now very much a part of the wired world.

And just-in-time manufacturing, when coordinated through the Internet, is reshaping how we deal with distance. Once manufacturers find that more of their orders come in via the Net, especially orders that carry some level of customization, then suddenly JIT doesn't easily fit with old-style distribution methods. When your customers no longer order a truckload of products at a time, it's difficult to contract with trucking companies for regular runs. It's tough to order railcars for cross-country shipments when you've only produced a handful of items. The old ways of dealing with products and distances don't fit anymore.

People want just a few parts and they want them now. Orders are smaller, there are more of them, and they carry a greater urgency.

Internet distance means this: JIT orders can be placed with any manufacturer, anywhere on the planet, as long as that manufacturer can deliver that order as fast as anyone else. If a manufacturer a continent away can produce a part just as fast as the business down the street, it has set itself up as a viable competitor. This is an important lesson to carry with you as you move from basic training to battle mode. **Today, being near a rail line or a major trucking hub may be less important than being near a key hub for an overnight service. Small packages and quick turnaround times rule the day.**

Another change is found on the education front. Distance learning has been an important advance for some schools. It has made it possible for schools to aggregate, say, kids in six towns who want to learn Latin. If there were only three students in each school with that interest, it would never be cost-effective to hire a teacher for each school. And it might be costly to bus kids back and forth and take too big a bite out of the school day. But distance learning, with video, shared whiteboards, and messaging centers, makes it possible to gather 18 remote students to hold the class. The schools can be hundreds of miles apart.

Distance ceases to matter. New opportunities in languages, sciences, everything, are available to students as distance compresses.

Distance can also mean something radically different than the traditional physical sense. Manufacturers can feel distanced from a market. For example, makers of aftermarket auto radios can feel distanced from a market if a car's design makes it difficult to retrofit one of their products. (Take a look at the late 1990s Ford Taurus models. The radio is oval. How easy is it to buy a replacement at your local Circuit City?)

There are even ways to create distance that you need to watch for. Sometimes it's very difficult to serve a specific market segment without a lot of extra planning and work. The Internet itself can effectively distance some suppliers from new markets. Even if you can do things more efficiently, you may be unable to effectively replace a vendor who has locked a customer into a proprietary technology that allows that vendor to seamlessly integrate into the customer's computer system. You can't step in and offer a similar service without thousands of work hours. The Internet may be open, but a proprietary flavor of it can close you out.

Likewise, that vendor may be unable to compete with you if you integrate better, open standard systems that shuffle all data via the Extensible Markup Language (XML), a model for describing data that's becoming a basic building block for databases and documents. Using XML, you could undercut the other vendor's expensive proprietary solution, and gain new business quickly. In that case, a vendor's proprietary solution can effectively distance that company from new business.

And what about short distances? Previously, it didn't matter how close you were to a printer if you didn't have a printer cable. It didn't matter how close you were to a vending machine if you didn't have proper change (or at least a sledgehammer). But now we have Bluetooth short-distance wireless technology, and even short distances have changed.

Bluetooth is an open standard for short-range transmission of digital voice and data. It's usually used between mobile devices (laptops,

PDAs, phones) and networked devices, from desktop computers, to network connections, to vending machines. It was developed by the Bluetooth Special Interest Group (www.bluetooth.com), founded by Ericsson, IBM, Intel, Nokia, and Toshiba. A Bluetooth modem sits on a desk and talks to a laptop computer in any room of your home. Bluetooth-enabled PCs and printers can work together without having a wired connection between the two devices. It's better than infrared connections because it doesn't have infrared's line-of-sight limits. Instead, it's a tiny radio transmission. Cell phones can talk to vending machines—providing debit-card information. The computer in your office or at home in your den can sync with your handheld devices without having to drop the handheld in a docking cradle. And you can even sync with your wife and children's handheld organizers around the breakfast table.

Internet time. Internet distance. They are esoteric concepts to comprehend or measure, but they have restructured the way we think of everything. **A competitive company is one that has learned to use Internet time to its advantage. A company on the move is one that has learned to use Net technologies to compress distance in order to save time and money. A company on the rise is one that has learned to do both in order to remove inefficiencies from its operation.**

Landslides, Land Mines, and Liquid Inventory— The New Competitive Terrain

Mastering the tools that compress time and distance can bring you new business. If you do it well, maybe even a landslide of new business. When that happens, you have to leverage your knowledge of the Net to efficiently ramp up your operation without dropping a single order. The more open and standards-based your operation, the easier it is for you to integrate with new partners. The easier it is for you to share data, the easier it will be for you to smooth the road between those you buy from and those you sell to. You will be a middleman who adds value.

Not being able to ramp quickly can affect the trajectory of your business. **Being locked into a limited, proprietary system that's difficult to integrate with other systems is like hitting a land mine on your path to success. It can stop you cold. Hurt you. Cost you a winning move.**

But you can ride the landslide and avoid the land mines by remaining liquid. You do this by working in concert with the flow of information that affects your business. As we stress through this book, every product flows in stages, from raw material to finished product to consumer. It doesn't matter if the product is a machine part, a music recording, or a cup of coffee, the market process follows a similar path. Seamlessly connecting every link in the chain, and empowering those links to know what's happening upstream and down keeps the process flowing. The ultimate thing that you should keep liquid is your inventory. It's a big leap to let go and trust your supply chain via an automated e-procurement process. But you'll have to make that leap in order to eliminate the inefficiencies. It will be like hitting a land mine if you don't. Those who are able to leap over this obstacle will find a remarkably competitive advantage. Integration of supply chains changes the basic structure of how businesses compete in the new economy.

Today, products compete with other products and companies compete with other companies. Soon, integrated supply chains will compete with other supply chains to see who can be the most efficient.

In his book *Business at the Speed of Thought,* Bill Gates talks about establishing what he calls a digital nervous system that allows information to be shared openly across an organization, so that it can be absorbed and reacted to as needed. Just-in-time manufacturing systems, executed correctly, are a key example of this.

In just-in-time manufacturing, the more information you have about upcoming orders, the less inventory you need to store nearby in case of ramped up production. Dell computing reportedly keeps about eight days' worth of inventory on hand for all the parts it needs to construct its computers.

The digital nervous system Gates envisions, if it's possible, would extend from manufacturer to consumer, and it would likely allow a company like Dell to cut its inventory to just three or four days' worth of products on the shelf.

But you can't shoot for such efficiencies right out of the gate. **The easiest way to get started in e-procurement is to concentrate first on buying goods that aren't used directly in production.** This can be office supplies, or maintenance, repair, and operations (MRO) products. Work the kinks out of your system there, and then move on to the production items most likely to reduce your production costs. From there, you can experiment with getting lower prices through tactics like reverse auctions and publicly posted RFPs and RFQs.

How to Read the Lay of the Land When All You See Is a Computer Screen

The Internet has given us a remarkable window into everything in the universe. This window can be as wide as we want it to be, or it can be narrowed to focus on specific niches. Sometimes the most important window is the one that shows us exactly what we need to know as we make our daily decisions.

The problem is, to view this window, we've had to sit at a desk, staring at a computer screen, one step removed from the physical world that the data represents. Yes, you can look at your screen to see that you have 100 boxes in your warehouse. But you could see the same thing if you were in that warehouse. What's more, if you were away from your desk and walking the aisles, you might see other things that a manager needs to see, like a leaky roof or workers who take two-hour lunch breaks.

Our reliance on supply chain data increasingly requires us to stay plugged in. Thank goodness the effort to place wireless PCs in the palm of our hands has come along on the heels of the Internet to free

us from our desks so we can take the data with us. We can manage by walking around, and still be free to check any fact we need.

Digital cell phones capable of receiving text pages were a start down this road, as were Palm computers capable of syncing with desktop systems so we could take mail, calendars, and notes with us. But we wanted more.

Taking the data with you, getting out, talking with others, building relationships is what will really help you read the lay of the land and the pulse of the marketplace. There is no substitute. You also need to remain connected, via a desktop computer, to communities on the Web. Rather than reading just your data stream, participate in the clubs and the message boards that deal with your business. These sources help you connect to others like yourself who will provide you with valuable information.

PART TWO

preparation

maximize your organization:
focus on posture

as a company grows, the scope of what leaders must deal with changes. This is true whether you are commanding a troop of soldiers or a company of modern workers. Today, growth is inevitable in companies doing their business right. Good sound management practices are universal and should not change as the company swells. From the top down, the issue is still about managing a small group of people. You start with a small group of employees. Later, you manage a small group of supervisors, then a small group of directors, and then a small group of vice presidents. In turn, each manages his or her own small group, tasked with reaching goals in line with the vision established at the top.

Each small group must know who its internal and external customers are. They must know what their product or service is, and be dedicated to improving it, even as workflow changes.

Some of the toughest issues for a larger company are coordinating product development across multiple departments, creating distribution systems for multiple products, and coordinating marketing efforts for those multiple products. Establishing proper lines of communication, a reporting structure, and a shared online schedule are ways to keep the chaos under control.

Fast-lane Internet companies that rely on their employees' creativity can grow quickly when they target the right business niche. But that growth can be very complicated. If not properly managed, it can drag on the company's efficacy. This highlights one of the major problems faced by start-up companies or fast-moving divisions of established companies. **Creative people create, organized people manage, and one group is not always thinking about the concerns of the other.** Yet they should be.

Creating a product with no concern for company standards, management practices, or business needs is a recipe for disaster. Hampering creative development by not supporting new technologies or ideas is also a recipe for failure in a thriving, fast-paced economy. Merging the concerns of both sides is tough, but waiting until product launch to address such issues is disastrous. **The integration of creativity with the structures and rules of technology is paramount.**

The better, faster, cheaper mantra should be known to all, but a commitment to better (meaning quality) must be paramount. Make sure your creative folks, the people designing and building the product, focus on standards, quality, and process management from the start. As you prepare to do battle for new business, this orientation is an important step toward being prepared for quick expansion.

It's tough to tell a bunch of dedicated people who work long hours that they need to step back and also help establish the important business processes needed for product management. That business process does not immediately benefit them. It benefits the people who will manage the product after they create it.

But it comes back to the key question of this chapter. What is the *posture* of your organization? Is it to ramp up quickly with a new idea, and then sell it to the highest bidder? If so, then letting the creative people run free might not be a bad thing. But if you plan to manage and market the product you create, then quality monitoring, documentation, and managing a timetable for deliverables is most important. As you expand into e-commerce, know where you best plug into the money stream. Are you focused on order taking? Payment processing? Inventory tracking? Fulfillment?

If you are a media company, is your goal to build a long-term Web presence and build traffic? Is it to create a specific community of buyers and sellers in which total page views don't matter, because money is made as items change hands? Do you want to aggregate page views at your site? Or do you prefer to supply content to multiple sites? Is establishing your brand more important than revenue for the short term?

A commitment to quality, efficiency, and timeliness is a commitment that must be set by the leaders in every organization. The message needs to be conveyed to every worker at every level. It can be easier to do this by adhering to a set, recognized structure, like a total quality management (TQM) process, or an extremely tight quality standard like Sigma Six. When these are in place, employees know what is expected, and everyone in the organization can be called upon to deliver that quality. Few start-up companies worry about such standards, but they should be a future goal because they mark your company as successful in its efforts to get its process under control.

The Internet land-grab economy, after its tremendous and reckless growth spurt, won't survive without some serious reengineering. This may seem strange to folks who think the reengineering fad and things like TQM are passé. TQM focuses on obtaining continuous feedback for making improvements and refining existing processes over the long term. That's never a bad thing. TQM efforts failed in many companies in the early 1990s because the feedback was overly manual and not continuous, and adjustments were not always made when the feedback showed a problem. TQM requires constant monitoring and adjustment, and was usually declared a failure by companies who could not maintain the effort it required. Today, such feedback loops can be automated and better communication established via Net technologies.

A recent survey by Bain & Co., a Boston management consulting firm, listed the most popular management tools and techniques for executives in large companies. TQM and reengineering ranked roughly in the middle of the pack for usage and satisfaction. Interestingly, they have lingered on lists like this for years, while other top-ranked techniques have come and gone.

Other timeless essentials for management include:
- **Comprehensive strategic-planning sessions with key employees**
- **Mission and vision statements (outlining exactly what the company's mission and vision are, with buy-in from all employees)**
- **Benchmarking (standardized tasks that test the capabilities of devices, processes, or services, used to set a standard for response times and accuracy)**
- **Customer-satisfaction measurements**

ISO 9000 and Buzzword Compliance

Besides establishing internal management techniques to shepherd your company's growth, it may be important for you to participate in more widely recognized management systems. **Every army has its rules and regulations: So does technology.** ISO is the International Organization for Standardization, based in Geneva, Switzerland. The U.S. member of ISO is the American National Standards Institute (ANSI).

Founded in the mid-1940s, ISO deals with most manufacturing standards except for electrical and electronics, which are governed by the International Electrotechnical Commission (IEC). ISO comprises hundreds of technical committees and thousands of subcommittees tasked with analyzing technical issues faced by companies, and recommending standards that assure quality and compatibility. Such standards help the international exchange of goods and services. More important, they promote trust in the quality of goods sold.

In the computer industry, ISO created the seven-layer OSI (Open Systems Interconnection) model that has influenced software design and communications. But that's not the standard that will put bread on your .com table.

As you move into e-commerce and supply chain management, the standard that affects many manufacturers, software developers, and systems integrators is ISO 9000. This is a family of standards and guidelines for establishing quality practices in manufacturing and service industries. It basically defines what should be measured, and documents the processes for companies working toward certification. Many companies will only partner with ISO 9000–certified companies. **Gaining ISO certification is one way to show you are moving beyond the seat-of-the-pants start-up phase, and working toward serious, standardized business practices.**

A major update to the standard was released mid-December 2000. It's a structural and strategic revision that streamlines how the standard is implemented. If you haven't looked at the standard in a while, the new ISO 9000: 2000 is one reason to do so. Even if you're not the kind of organization that needs ISO 9000, there is much you can learn from the concept.

ISO 9000 explains criteria for what should be measured.

ISO 9001 sets requirements, details product design and development.

ISO 9002 (now obsolete) spanned production, installation, and service.

ISO 9003 (now obsolete) covered practices for final testing and inspection.

ISO 9004 establishes guidance for performance improvement— now consolidated into four main sections
- Management responsibility
- Resource management

- Product and/or service realization
- Measurement, analysis, and improvement

Details on the 2000 update can be found at www.iso.ch/9000e/revisionstoc.htm.

Another buzz phrase that's fallen in and out of fashion but is relevant in the e-world is Six Sigma. (Fewer than four defects per million parts manufactured.) Only a few manufacturers are capable of attaining this level of quality. Yet those who strive for this see not only increased sales, but also significant internal costs savings because of reduced returns and fewer service issues.

Six Sigma actually has eight stages, effectively redesigning everything a company does rather than finding and correcting errors and defects. Its goal, rather than providing a quality monitoring approach, is to keep you from making mistakes in the first place. Could you achieve this? Could you then extend this capability down the supply chain to include subassembly and component suppliers? Could you track all this via the Net? If you don't, you will not achieve the level of quality you demand.

As e-commerce evolves, keep an eye on one final standards effort called Collaborative Planning, Forecasting, and Replenishment (CPFR). The concept was developed by the Interindustry Commerce Standards Association. The idea is for companies participating in a supply chain to outline their business concept and develop a scorecard to track appropriate supply chain metrics. They also establish shared financial rewards or penalties for hitting or missing specific targets. From there, the concept works on developing a joint business plan, collaborative sales forecasting, and order and inventory forecasting. CPFR is still too new to have a huge following, but its ambitions are noteworthy.

The posture of your organization is your level of commitment. It is your ability to set a goal and work toward it and the ability of leaders to instill confidence in everyone that the goal will be attained because all the processes are in place and the full organization is committed to quality. But can such a commitment to process and structure be at odds with the creative, fast-paced, do-it-now edifice of an Internet company? Such new-economy organizations need to create a risk-taking, reward-driven environment. That's how to keep your best people working for you.

Building on a Solid Foundation

Once you have the basic management techniques established, the tools in place, quality issues under control, and costs properly in check, it's simply a matter of organization to keep the supervisory machine moving so that productivity stays high.

In the military, keeping the war machine moving is actually a matter of establishing the proper logistics. It takes at least 10 soldiers to properly supply every soldier on the front lines. That number rises when the battle is farther from home. The best situation for a fighting soldier is to be able to reach behind him and find whatever tool or weapon he needs. Someone is right there, handing him the keys to victory. In the modern business world, the approach is similar. Give your employees what they need to succeed. Give your customers what they want, when they need it. Even better, before they need it.

This capability starts with following accepted business practices, and branches out to proper goal setting and communication with employees. Where the *posture* of the organization takes you, eventually, is into that all-important realm of logistics.

What you need to establish is the logistics of the workplace, from work-flow to information flow to who does what, when, and why. This is fantastically important. Yet in a fast-paced .com economy, this aspect of business is often overlooked. It's understandable. There is an urgency to get it out the door and then worry about other parts of the business later.

But building any product without a business plan is risky. Yes, there are some winners. Shawn Fanning reportedly envisioned a solution to a music file-sharing problem while riding in a car. He promptly ignored his college classes and lived on a diet of pizza for a month so he could construct the marvelous music-sharing program known as Napster. Marc Andreessen had a similar epiphany when he constructed the first Web browser, Mosaic, then turned that product into Netscape and became a multimillionaire. But how many of us can take that "develop the product now, develop the business plan later" attitude? College kids, who are already poor and desperate, are about the only ones who can afford that kind of risk.

Set the business plan. Set the logistics to make that plan happen. Set a process for checking the quality of goods and services. Then build and distribute the product. Early in its life cycle, confirm that all parts are in place to maintain the posture of your organization. These will give you the right foundation from which to build.

Shaking the Tree, Digging in the Dirt

One formula that works in many situations, after you've set your work structure and your quality control, is to commit your normal, reliable workers to your everyday tasks, and save your most talented workers for special projects and efforts. This is no different from a general in battle who uses normal forces to engage the enemy and special forces for extraordinary tasks that lead to a big win.

Surprisingly, the best results can sometimes come from having your special forces concentrate on projects that allow you to go after the ever-popular low-hanging fruit. These are the easy wins that fill your coffers and build your value and power. Why target the special forces there? Why not save them for the big play, and target your standard workforce at the low-hanging fruit? Because it's vitally important that you win these battles, even though they are small. In a war, armies don't immediately target the most heavily fortified installations. They hit the weak points. They go where they can win and keep winning, building victorious momentum.

This combination of sustained and special applications builds a company's momentum, like a flood's rising water that moves seemingly immovable boulders. **The momentum of a corporation skilled in the art of business development can be likewise overwhelming because its deals, movements, and market announcements are precisely timed.** A business that successfully executes this wavelike rhythm, with a good product and good management, is like a fully drawn crossbow. The potential is there. Good targeting and good timing are all that's needed to make the weapon work.

> **In** the chaotic uproar of the Net, there is too much tolerance for chaos. There can be no disorder in your workers or in your business plan. Proper execution is everything.

Keep in mind that your opponents, likewise, will be poised to strike at the proper moment. Don't make it easy for them. Don't make your plans so obvious they will be able to base their decisions on what you do. Fool them. **Look disorganized and unready to advance when you are very organized. Look like you are not ready to complete projects or enter into new deals, even when you're on the brink of completing a major new partnership.**

This is difficult for a public company, which needs to be straightforward in its dealings. It also must satisfy its stockholders, who need to know that the ship is on an even keel.

The only way to successfully fool and mislead is to be very organized and deliberate within your organization. It is only possible to mislead people about your plans when you have a definite plan upon which your workers are focused. If your true intentions and business focus are known by your own people, then your full organization will know both the importance of the mission and the consequence of letting the world know, too soon, what that mission is.

In a battle, a significant strategic advantage is held by the leader who can make his opponent react. It's an advantage when you want to flush out and defeat a smaller, weaker enemy, and it's an advantage when you want to annoy and test the strength of a stronger enemy. Leaders skilled in making an opponent react usually do so by creating a specific situation they can control, which causes the kind of reaction they anticipate. Yet they do nothing to tip their own hand nor cause any worry to stockholders.

At the height of the Cold War, American and Soviet jets were constantly flying near each other's borders, often right up to and along the edge of whatever recognized border the two agreed to observe. In many cases, a half-mile closer would have been considered an invasion of the other country's air space. Some of the best tests were conducted along the Bering Sea between Alaska and the Kamchatka and Chukchi peninsulas of Russia, but the game was also played along Eastern Europe borders.

The trick wasn't actually to cross the line, though that was done occasionally to see if the other side detected the intrusion. The real goal was to draw a reaction from the opponent. Did they send a jet to intercept? Did they send more than one? How quickly could they catch up? Who triggered whose radar first? Were any holes found in the border that didn't seem fully covered by radar? Did the enemy paint the jet, locking on a targeting system to show they had the capability to shoot the jet down if they wanted? How easily could the jet itself lock onto that targeting radar, sending a missile back down the beam to destroy the enemy's radar installation?

For more than three decades, thousands of such border flights were made for one purpose—to force the other side to react. It was a cat-and-mouse game that helped each side judge the power, speed, and capabilities of the other. At the same time, a very similar game was being played under the sea in nuclear submarines.

Of course, each side knew their reaction was being judged, so they had to decide just how much they would reveal about their abilities when reacting to each threat. Too weak a reaction, and they might not look capable. Too strong, and the other side might decide they should spend more money on defense, upgrade their systems, and make themselves more threatening.

In business, to properly deceive an opponent, a situation must be created with proper knowledge of how the other company or person usually reacts. You can entice the opponent with something you know they want. This can be a potential partnership, a sliver of a particular market they desire, a special technology they want to develop, or an industry effort in which they'd like to participate. You can judge their reactions. Did they do what you thought they would? If not, why? Do they have something else in development? Can you discover what this is? Can you keep your opponent on the move by holding out such bait, while concentrating your most reliable and talented workers on your own special projects?

One of the best ways to keep tabs on your competition is to allow your employees to monitor discussion panels at trade shows and to participate in standardization efforts for your industry. They will hear what employees of other organizations support, and why. They may hear early mentions of new projects. Names will be dropped. Hints of intentions will be floated.

With this glint of information, you can start drawing a map of the direction your competition is taking.

To take advantage of such details, you must be certain of your own abilities even if you are not fully sure of your opponent's. To compare and contrast capabilities, you must have confidence in your organization, know and trust your own qualities. Your employees must share that confidence. This is why the posture of the organization is so important. People know where they stand. You've established processes, built them, tested them, and they work. Confidence, good organization, and a clear mission make you a powerful foe.

Part of posture may mean compassion. A skilled leader exploits situations, not people. He or she capitalizes a situation, but doesn't demand, unless it's highly necessary, a direct attack or unreasonable sacrifices like long hours, low pay, and other stressful situations. When you focus on exploiting a situation, but not people, you retain respect for humanity. When you focus on the situation, you can utilize the proper people in your organization much more effectively than you can for a long-term, unfocused buildup.

Remember the wave approach. If you focus always on your overall momentum rather than executing quickly to take advantage of a specific situation, you end up rolling boulders rather than throwing punches. **In the long run, the boulder may carry more power. But it's difficult to get started and difficult to aim. It's harder on your people. A well-timed punch may be more effective for winning a limited, but important battle, and it might be less taxing on your workers.**

The most competitive large organizations never forget the value of those limited, short-term gains as a key to success. In the fall of 2000, while Microsoft was in the midst of fighting its monopoly accusations from the Justice Department and focusing on an update to its Windows 2000 system, it still found time to chase after and prosecute vendors of counterfeit software in Florida and extend itself even further into the B2B space by expanding its agreement to integrate its commerce platform with Commerce One's e-marketplace infrastructure. Big company. Small victories. Steady gains.

If you are winning battles, time is on your side. As your organization grows, you will be able to dedicate people to focus on both long-term momentum and short-term gain.

The Demands of Leadership

Leadership, in business, is a strange mix of vision, hard work, and attention to detail. Of the three, attention to detail may be the most important. Are your databases updated routinely, or only when you discover data has become unreliable? Do you follow up with additional information or problem solving when you say you will, or are promises forgotten? Do you delegate responsibilities when demands become too numerous, and do you check to see that those details were indeed handled by others?

The efficient, detail-oriented, results-driven leader is an important pivot point for .combat and your organization. Even if she isn't the type who talks tough and makes boastful promises, even if she isn't the type who is constantly quoted on the evening news, the leader can set the tone for the whole enterprise.

In the sixth century, Chinese poet Lao-tzu summarized the essence of good leadership this way

> A leader is best
> When people barely know he exists,
> Not so good when people obey and acclaim him,
> Worse when they despise him.
> But of a good leader, who talks little,
> When his work is done, his aim fulfilled,
> They will say:
> We did it ourselves.

Lao-tzu's summation is the not the Hollywood version of a great warrior. It's not the mark of someone who fights hard, wins big, and wallows in the spoils of war. But it is the mark of someone who succeeds. It's someone who leads by example, sets up a structure by which others can succeed, and then allows competent people to do their jobs.

The most dangerous leader to compete with is the one you don't notice. Perhaps he's the guy you ride next to on the train every day as he slowly builds an empire. Such a man can slip across borders totally undetected. He's the invisible man. He's the kind of guy who discovers the right information for the right business opportunity because no one thinks twice about sharing it with him.

We need such a leader, even if we don't look up to him.

We tend to look up to a different sort of person. We admire the Ted Turners, the Larry Ellisons, and the Scott McNealys of the world. But it's often the quieter, steadfast leader who has the greatest long-term impact.

A perfect example of the quieter, highly organized, and tremendously effective leader in today's corporate world is probably Jack Welch, the longtime CEO of General Electric. While you can't deny that Welch has been high-profile during his tenure, he was not the type who actively sought the limelight. It was mainly Welch's competitive nature, dogged work, and stunning success at growing GE revenues and share value that kept the spotlight on him and his accomplishments.

Welch was a detail guy. He wanted his employees to be detail-oriented people because it meant a quality organization and higher-quality products. In the mid-1990s, Welsh's attention to detail drew him to the Six Sigma concept mentioned previously.

Likewise, when Welsh committed to move into e-business, he did it in a big way. In 1999, he asked top executives in major business units to devise detailed e-business strategies in little more than a single quarter. The goal was to establish key interfaces to customers and suppliers to streamline the transaction process. By 2000, GE handled about $5 billion of business online, according to a *Forbes* magazine estimate. Some GE managers have touted that, by using a Web interface to track most purchasing and sales, they can shave 20 percent or more off the cost of selling and also off general and administrative expenses.

Welch boasted to shareholders that e-business would "change the DNA of GE forever by energizing and revitalizing every corner of this company." In reality, his corporation was revitalized by a very detail-oriented individual who knew the value of hard work, and who could make a strong commitment to catch up when he saw his organization falling behind the e-business curve. **Inspiring workers to rally behind an important cause is a quality that every great leader needs. In the e-world, that talent is increasingly important.**

Historic Perspective and Future Directive

To understand why management techniques have shifted in the Internet age, it's important to know how management evolved over the past

200 years. Those involved in the media or entertainment side of the Net may think these concepts don't apply to them. But they do. Businesses revolve around products or services even if the product is a digital video broadcast, and even if the service is editing music or creating Web graphics. Lessons from the manufacturing floor are lessons for everyone.

Prior to the Industrial Revolution, goods were mainly produced by people who used hand tools. Manufacturing was small scale, by people who made items in their homes, barns, and village shops. People realized that goods made in shops could be produced in larger numbers. Sometimes workers would produce enough pieces to assemble five or 10 units at a time. By the mid-1800s, steam power helped the wheels of industry spin faster. It became more efficient for one person to do nothing but create parts while others worked on assembling the parts. Manufacturing operations were consolidated under ever-larger roofs. Manufacturing became a process rather than a discrete event, and parts of this process had to be supervised on a scale that small shops never needed. The midlevel manager was born.

This structure was new to business, but not to the military, where midlevel managers in the form of junior officers had been the norm for centuries. Business owes much of its basic organization to military concepts.

As factories grew in size, larger, more complex items were manufactured, and the manufacturing process itself grew in complexity. Efficiency was needed, and the role of supervisors rose in importance. They are the ones who identify and trim waste. Eventually the concept of specialization was introduced. Just as stone masons, carpenters, goldsmiths, and other craftsmen were specialists before the Industrial Revolution, the Industrial Revolution brought with it a need for many new types of specialists and tradesmen. As both products and processes grew more complex, the need arose to automate shop functions. This also meant automating the flow of information in the shop and in the business office. At first, sharing information was as simple as writing on a box or an item as it traveled through the factory. It progressed to clipboards, chalkboards, vacuum tubes, and eventually computer systems set up to track parts and predict needs.

Traditionally, information technology in the factory focused on improving the manufacturing process and increasing workers' efficiency, while information technology in offices focused on orders, billing, and payments. The rise of Internet technologies made it possible for both systems to talk to each other, even if they're on different computer platforms. Today, factory floor data and office data are merging. They are even merging with external information from buyers, suppliers, partners, and consultants. Your "factory" could be the database you build or even the video or music you create. But the entertainment industry has yet to establish the end-to-end process control seen in other businesses.

Where does your company fit in this new river of data? Does the posture of your organization place you in the middle of this flood? If it does, are you seaworthy or headed for a wreck?

Because it's possible to purchase items directly over the Internet, the online sales angle of the Internet revolution has been the focus of most manufacturers. But the process is much more involved than just sales. It's the sharing of inventory information, the prediction tools, and the ability to track time and costs across multiple organizations. These are the functions that show the true value of e-commerce systems. More attention is now turned to improving the performance and productivity of the decision makers throughout an organization. Manufacturing information systems pull their information directly from the production process, tracking everything from raw materials to numbers of finished products produced. Everyone from purchasing managers to the accounts payable department can access the data. These changes apply to all types of businesses. In fact, the entertainment industry should be extremely concerned with tracking mechanisms because they are key to digital rights management, which helps control piracy and confirms that owners get paid for their work.

> **Inefficiency still runs rampant in all businesses. If you can create a system that squeezes even a little inefficiency out of a system by using collected data, there is a place for your product in today's e-commerce battlefield.**

Despite the radical changes that information technology has carried into the manufacturing process, despite the fact that e-commerce has opened a vast new competitive terrain that we're only beginning to explore, the rules of how to keep an organization on track have not changed that much since ancient times. To close this chapter, here are some lessons that still apply and prove that the competitive posture of an organization is set by educated leaders.

Sun Tzu says:

1. **"The control of a large force is the same principle as the control of a few men; it is merely a question of dividing up their numbers."**

2. **"Fighting with a large army under your command is no different from fighting with a small one; it is merely a question of instituting signs and signals."**

In this chapter we discuss the complexity faced by a growing organization. Meticulous attention to details and proper methods for supervising the supervisors in a small group keeps the organization under control. With an organization of approximately 37,000 workers, Sun Microsystems CEO Scott McNealy limits his direct reports to about five. With a GE empire of 340,000 workers, Jack Welch has about 25 direct reports.

This means more than keeping the lines of communication open at every level of your organization, via the supervisors. It includes open sharing of data with your supervisors to empower their decision making.

3. "To ensure that your whole host may withstand the brunt of the enemy's attack and remain unshaken—this is effected by maneuvers direct and indirect."

In modern business terms, know your organization, and empower your organization to know itself. Create teams that work well together. Create teams that react quickly to change and challenge. And make sure the teams have the information they need to make their decisions. Make sure they work together and are comfortable with each other, strong, and capable. Recall the early lessons in this chapter. You have to be organized and effective before you can successfully feign ineffectiveness.

4. "That the impact of your army may be like a grindstone dashed against an egg—this is effected by the science of weak points and strong."

If your organization is effective, efficient, and highly competitive, you will always win the struggle for market space. Developing the right information system and sharing that information internally and with partners is one of the best ways to remain highly efficient and stronger than your competitors.

5. "In all fighting, the direct method may be used for joining battle, but indirect methods will be needed in order to secure victory."

Create situations that cause your opponent to react. If the wisest leader is indeed one who can win without fighting, then the indirect method of conflict (spying and reconnaissance) is as important, if not more important, than the direct method. Again, Net technologies are powerful tools to exploit indirect methods. There is no more efficient reconnaissance vehicle available today.

6. "Indirect tactics, efficiently applied, are inexhaustible as Heaven and Earth, unending as the flow of rivers and streams; like the Sun and Moon, they end but to begin anew; like the four seasons, they pass away to return once more."

As you realize the effectiveness of your efforts—be they watching your opponent from afar, or developing internal processes for operational efficiency—you will fall into a routine of tapping into the information flow to analyze and adjust without direct confrontation.

7. "There are not more than five musical notes, yet the combinations of these five give rise to more melodies than can ever be heard."

8. "There are not more than five primary colors (blue, yellow, red, white, and black), yet in combination they produce more hues than can ever be seen."

9. "There are not more than five cardinal tastes (sour, acrid, salt, sweet, and bitter), yet combinations of them yield more flavors than can ever be tasted."

10. "In battle, there are not more than two methods of attack—the direct and the indirect; yet these two in combination give rise to an endless series of maneuvers."

11. "The direct and the indirect lead on to each other in turn. It is like moving in a circle—you never come to an end. Who can exhaust the possibilities of their combination?"

These truths advise knowing when the time is right, and acting on it. You gain knowledge through your indirect methods. You read the news, you read your opponents' sales materials. If you have limited partnerships, you learn how seriously partners take their efforts, and how they treat customers. You learn, watch, and wait. When the time arrives for the direct conflict—for the detailed sales pitch or answering a request for bid—your indirect operations will support your major decisions. You find the right combination and make it work.

12. "The onset of troops is like the rush of a torrent, which will even roll stones along in its course."

13. "The quality of decision is like the well-timed swoop of a falcon, which enables it to strike and destroy its victim."

14. "Therefore, the good fighter will be terrible in his onset, and prompt in his decision."

15. "Energy may be likened to the bending of a crossbow; decision, to the releasing of a trigger."

When you know yourself and your opponent, you are certain what to do when you find yourself in conflict. Move quickly and deliberately. Show your opponent just how deliberate and determined you can be. A good plan, properly executed, is a marvelous deterrent when you compete against a poorly organized opponent who is not confident.

16. "Amid the turmoil and tumult of battle, there may be seeming disorder and yet no real disorder at all; amid confusion and chaos, your array may be without head or tail, yet it will be proof against defeat."

17. "Simulated disorder postulates perfect discipline; simulated fear postulates courage; simulated weakness postulates strength."

18. "Hiding order beneath the cloak of disorder is simply a question of subdivision; concealing courage under a show of timidity presupposes a fund of latent energy; masking strength with weakness is to be effected by tactical dispositions."

Soldiers have long mentioned the fog of war where plans break down in a battle, and confusion reigns. But even in confusion, an organization that knows itself and its abilities should rise above the other and enter the end game to finish the conflict. In the fast, furious evolution of Internet markets, it's tough to know what to focus on and where to invest money and effort. It could all be lost when a new technology emerges or a new market space evolves! But an organization that's confident in its abilities, and confident that it can judge and react to change, should emerge a winner. Smart people don't risk all until they know they *can* win.

19. "Thus one who is skillful at keeping the enemy on the move maintains deceitful appearances, according to which the enemy will act. He sacrifices something, that the enemy may snatch at it."

20. "By holding out baits, he keeps the enemy on the march; then with a body of picked men he lies in wait for him."

Remember the Cold War antics and border tests between the Soviets and the United States? Both sides were artful at deceiving and testing each other. Likewise, to win a space in the evolving e-marketplaces, you must first judge which are the most valuable spaces to occupy. You may need to deceive others as you lay your plans, so they won't realize you've identified the biggest slice of the pie.

21. "The clever combatant looks to the effect of combined energy, and does not require too much from individuals. Hence his ability to pick out the right men and utilize combined energy."

22. "When he utilizes combined energy, his fighting men become as it were like unto rolling logs or stones. For it is the nature of a log or stone to remain motionless on level ground, and to move when on a slope; if four-cornered, to come to a standstill, but if round-shaped, to go rolling down."

At first, this sounds like advice to keep all your eggs in one basket, or all your warriors in one squad. But the real lesson is to execute quickly and deliberately, even if it means pulling your best people off other jobs to participate in a focused effort. This may mean working hard to get a key piece of software out the door, or shutting down and refocusing a manufacturing group for a week while you rearrange and network the shop floor. Sometimes the best way to accomplish a goal is to throw all your resources at it to get it done quickly.

23. "Thus the energy developed by good fighting men is as the momentum of a round stone rolled down a mountain thousands of feet in height."

develop your offensive strategy

The Case for Corporate Espionage

In war, there are spies. And as I showed you earlier, there is a place in .combat for spying.

In the Cold War, the spy held a special place in our hearts, from Johnny Rivers singing "Secret Agent Man" to James Bond working his special magic. We truly believed that the right spy, in the right place, at the right time, could actually save the world.

Spies have a job to do. We picture the spy as a hero who risks all and ends up doing the job of an entire army all by himself. But there is another kind of spy, too. The spy of convenience. This is the person who knows something and can be bought or befriended and slowly turned into a spy. This type of spy was a favorite of ancient generals, including Sun Tzu.

Today, ethical questions swirl around the use of corporate spies. What seemed perfectly reasonable in the winner-take-all fog of war somehow seems underhanded, slightly wrong, and downright illegal in the gentlemanly realm of business. Yet corporate spying is as old as corporations themselves. There is always a need to know what your competition is up to, and the ways to find that out many times fall into a questionable gray area. Perhaps the problem is with the name itself. Espionage is a more polite word than spying. "Competitive-intelligence professional" is perhaps the most respectable term.

Don't doubt that such people exist. There's even a Society of Competitive Intelligence Professionals (SCIP) in Alexandria, Virginia. It claims nearly 7,000 members, 25 percent of them from outside the United States. Some companies have full departments dedicated to intelligence gathering. Screw the cost. Not having the data costs more when you're making multimillion dollar decisions. I've even met officers from foreign militaries who admit they are developing new technologies that businesses in their countries can use.

A Real-Life Corporate Spy Story

In mid-2000, Oracle admitted that it hired a detective agency, Investigative Group International, to check out a pair of research organizations, the Independence Institute and the National Taxpayers Union. Oracle wanted to link Microsoft directly to these organizations during the Microsoft antitrust trial. Many accusations swirled around the investigation. Someone tried to buy trash bags. Someone's laptop computer turned up missing. How much of this was done by the private investigators is unclear.

Eventually Oracle concluded that the organizations were misrepresenting themselves as independent advocacy groups when they were at least partially funded by Microsoft. To Oracle CEO Ellison, that discovery justified the use of private eyes, even though he denied knowing ahead of time that they were being hired, or approving their use. "It is absolutely true we set out to expose Microsoft's covert activities," he said in a news conference just after the story broke. "I feel very good about what we did."

Ira Winkler, president of the Internet Security Advisors Group and the author of *Corporate Espionage,* reports that an average Fortune 500 firm gets spied on about four or five times a year. He said sometimes companies pay for information and do not want details on how it was obtained.

Any company that wants to find out what its competition is doing should be ready to pay a price. Espionage doesn't come cheap. Commercial industry reports can run tens of thousands of dollars. Large companies staff full departments devoted to competitive intelligence. Others hire consulting firms to collect and process important information. Companies who don't want to shoulder this expense may feel like they're saving money, but they need to ask themselves what they are paying for instead.

Sun Tzu writes in great detail about the cost of raising a hundred thousand men and marching them great distances. He writes about the financial costs, the emotional toll taken on families, the loss of life, and the pressure on the state. He also warns how hostile armies sometimes end up facing each other for years, spending valuable resources, striving for an important victory that might be decided in a single day. He writes all this, leading up to his question of why some leaders begrudge the outlay of a minor amount of money to pay for intelligence that could prevent that major effort and later expense. **To Sun Tzu, cutting costs on espionage is not a sign of leadership. It is a sign of ignorance.** It was the action of someone who knew nothing about the realities of gaining a victory, and who was willing to risk men instead of money. Today, some companies make the same mistake, choosing to save a few thousand dollars and not buy special industry reports or not subscribe to online services that analyze their marketplace. Further, they'd never consider directly hiring their own competitive-intelligence professionals. They spend more on product engineering and marketing than necessary, in order to play catch-up.

Your Own Crystal Ball

The ability to achieve goals that seem out of reach to most people is foreknowledge. It's knowing what will happen, what others will do, where the market is headed before anything happens.

Unfortunately, such foreknowledge cannot be divined from the spirit world, obtained from experiences you've not yet had, or derived from calculations, since you'll likely have little data to go on. Thus, knowledge of your opponent's dispositions can only be obtained from people and from select online sources.

Today, the Internet is the chief information-gathering vehicle for corporations. It's well ahead of direct spying. Such a wealth of competitive information can be gleaned from a site like Hoovers.com, that what a spy could offer pales in comparison. Yet, the spy might provide the missing piece of information that a thousand searches on Hoovers, which specializes in information about companies, won't turn up.

Not too many years ago you'd have to get on the telephone to track down a copy of a company's annual report or a Securities and Exchange Commission filing. **Now you can work with the SEC itself to receive e-mail notification of new filings, minutes after they arrive.**

While there are obvious competitive intelligence sites like Gartner and Forrester, sometimes data about your competition comes from unexpected places. For example, you can look at the logs on your Web server to see how often your competitor browses your site to collect info. **There's even a trick you can play on your competitors (think of it as counterintelligence) that uses domain-name identification and special site configuration. When a connection is detected from a competitor's domain name, those visitors can be diverted to special pages.** A major network router manufacturer was spotted using this trick to redirect competitors to specific pages, including a page about employment opportunities at the company. Of course, such surfers soon learned to use a different Web account than their employer's. (At least those AOL CD-ROMs turned out to be good for something besides drink coasters.)

The problem with any corporate intelligence-gathering operation is that your opponent will soon learn how you obtain your information if it's always from the same sources. Thus, you need to cultivate up to five types of spies, and use them all in varying degrees. Sun Tzu called this "divine manipulation of the threads." He means that this is a way of playing one information source against the other, reacting in different ways, and slowly judging which source is accurate.

- A local spy is one who inhabits the area around your opponent, or around the market that you want to conquer. Perhaps it's a person who rents an office in the same building. Maybe it's a cabdriver or a bartender. Information can be collected or purchased from these people. Trash bags can be obtained from a janitor. Trends can be spotted. You can get an early hint at new technologies or sales efforts.

- An inward spy is an actual employee of your competitor, or a controller of the market where you do business. These are very valuable spies. Hire them if you can. Or bribe them to tell you all they know. Hold business development meetings with them to learn their interests, how they structure a deal, how their money flows to partners, and what their traffic is.

- Converted spies are the opponent's own competitive-intelligence people. If you can enlist them, you'll discover they know more about you, and about your opponent, than you ever dreamed. If you can get a brain-dump from them, you'll have a remarkable asset. They are the most valuable catches.

- So-called doomed spies are pawns in a more elaborate game. Such a spy is one who is doomed to fail because he or she was discovered, and used. In such a case, a company may duplicitously do something, the wrong thing, openly in front of the intelligence gatherer. But it's done for purposes of deception. The spy will report back, and carry the wrong information.

- Surviving spies are ones who have actually been to your opponent's organization, who are able to bring back news. They have gone into the fray, met the opponent, seen the buildings and the people, and come out with a fresh perspective on the other organization.

There is no business you will engage in that's more important than building and maintaining intimate relationships with the right spies. Do not spare the rewards you give them for correct information. More information will follow. It may be better information. Do not brag to coworkers or friends at the golf club about your remarkably successful tactic. Be secretive about your actions. This is the dirtiest part of any business, and it's best left as a private matter.

Don't do anything illegal or in bad judgment. Be straightforward with paid spies. Let them know what you want and why. Be benevolent. But with other types of espionage, be cagey. Spies that you don't pay owe you nothing. They may report back to others on your actions and what you seek. Don't let on why you ask certain questions.

Hire experts to interpret reports. Things may not be as they seem. Multiple intelligence sources can confirm whether your intuition is correct, so always talk to more than one intelligence-gathering operative. Try to get four or five sources. Be subtle! Use multiple sources in a low-key way. Use them in every kind of business so your methods don't look unusual when you concentrate on a certain facet.

One type of basic research that often proves valuable is to find out the names of as many people as you can, from VPs to doorkeepers, from administrative assistants to product managers to programmers. At least know the names of your competitor's key managers. Even if you don't talk to these people directly, chances are you travel in the same circles on occasion. When the names come up, you'll know when to listen. And you may run into them at parties, where a few drinks will loosen their tongues. **Look for your competitors' employees who speak at trade shows. Listen to their sessions. Ask them questions without revealing your identity.**

There is more information out there than you realize. Information wants to be free on the Internet. Remember, the Net was developed by the military's Defense Advanced Research Projects Agency (DARPA) to assure that the United States has a communications system capable of surviving a nuclear war by automatically routing around computers that were suddenly missing from the network. That means the Net is capable of surviving the ultimate form of censorship—destruction.

Thus, nothing can really be censored on the Internet. If the information you want is out there, no one can stop you from obtaining it.

Remember that people are also spying on you. Seek out these watchers. Show them what you want them to see. Such contacts bring their own valuable information with them. Keep in mind that some of the most successful new companies were started by people who defected from other companies and brought contacts and intelligence with them. Find them and you will grow your own intelligence.

Develop an Offensive Strategy

The Internet land grab is essentially over. We are now in the consolidation phase.

The .com consolidation started as a trickle sometime in 1998, but it ramped up big-time in mid-2000 as venture capital and opportunities ran out for several fledgling companies. The shakeout could take two or three years to complete, maybe longer, since a continuous trickle of new Net technologies keeps extending the competitive battlefront into new areas like cutting-edge forms of wireless technology.

Anticipating consolidation is a key issue as you're planning your offensive strategy for the years ahead. Developing, investing in, or partnering to gain access to pivotal technologies is a great way to ride a wave toward development of new markets even if you don't have the option of becoming the big fish in the new pond. Your strategy may simply be to become a key technology or a key audience aggregator, making you a tasty morsel that the big fish wants to swallow. (It's also a strategy fraught with risk, since such markets may never emerge, and other technologies can supplant the one you thought was a winner.)

"It was predictable when the media model stopped working for a lot of people," said Lycos VP Sege. "First thing that happened—the stakes of marketing and reaching end users went up very high because the winners were spending $100 million per year. Folks who were less well capitalized couldn't afford that. They couldn't afford the ante to stay in the game and had to refocus. Many became ASPs. They said, 'What do we have that's valuable?' From database and application management to streaming technologies, they said, 'We can sell these to other .com companies.' That's how the whole ASP model first evolved."

As the consolidation became more ruthless, ASPs felt the pinch, too. "Some ASPs eventually said, 'Hey, we'll sell the whole company to you,' " said Sege. "If that didn't work, they started going out of business."

To survive, companies have to ask themselves if they can add value. Those that can't had bad business models to begin with.

Between the opportunity (or threat) of consolidation and the uncertainty of emerging technologies and markets, many small battles continue to loom on the front lines of Internet business development and technology. That's why it's important to develop a detailed offensive strategy as you proceed. If a battle seems certain for your company (and few companies can avoid occasional battles), you may need to adjust your business strategy, and take more of an offensive position to find opportunities and protect your current and future market position.

Yes, maintaining a proper defensive posture is also essential, and is explored in Chapter 4. But in a period of rapid change, like we see in the early years of this century, much greater strategic value comes from an offensive posture rather than standing still and hoping to defend yourself. If your only concern is defense, you may find yourself defending a technology or a market position that doesn't matter anymore.

The Auto Industry Parallel and Lessons Learned

The early days of the auto industry are a perfect example of this evolution and the way businesses effectively react to changing markets and new competition.

In 1769, a tinkerer named Nicolas Cugnot fitted a wagon with a rough steam engine and ran it across a field in France a few times before crashing it into a wall. Unfortunately (for horses anyway) technology adaptation didn't happen very fast back then, and it would be nearly 100 years before self-propelled wagons made a comeback. That resurrection was sparked by the development of a more efficient power source—the internal combustion engine.

An early engine was built in 1860 by Etienne Lenoir in France. It ran on a compressed gas and was never fully developed, but it was an idea whose time had come.

In 1877, German inventor Nikolaus August Otto invented the first truly successful internal combustion engine. With a new power source available, people began looking for work that could be performed with that power. The first thought was to attach the engine to industrial machinery. But taking the horse out of the horse-and-wagon mix was a priority for many people.

By 1886, Karl Benz created what's widely credited as the first automobile by attaching an engine of his own design to a three-wheeled cart. Over the next 10 years, several inventors started building and experimenting with similar engines and modifying horse wagons to create the genesis of an auto industry. The next step was to redesign the wagons to achieve better stability and endurance. The competition to build a better buggy began, and a new industry evolved.

The computer industry had a similar genesis. The first cumbersome commercial mainframes hit the market after World War II. It was a radical new technology in search of an application as computers migrated away from their first military jobs (cracking codes and calculating coordinates for artillery fire) toward office automation, where some people thought the machines' vast potential could truly be realized.

But in the early days of any market, a lack of knowledge prevails as to what that market will be. In 1943, Thomas J. Watson, then chairman of the board of International Business Machines, said, "I think there is a world market for maybe five computers." Likewise, early auto manufacturers aimed their inventions at the leisure class, rather than the working class, incorrectly assuming the main use for the vehicles was recreation. It took a few years for them to realize they were building something that would revolutionize transportation enough to become a must-have item for most households.

And things did progress. Higher speeds and heavier weights led to the development of better wheels and rubber tires. New steering mechanisms needed to be designed. New, associated markets developed as people built these related products and competed to supply the big manufacturers. Those who built the best tires or refined the best fuels became dominant players in these associated new industries.

But parallel technologies didn't disappear. Once a market settles on a key technology, price and market reach become more significant than developing a competing technology that does the same thing.

Henry Ford began experimenting with automobile design in the early 1880s. But he produced single or limited-production products until 1903. In 1908, he hit the jackpot when he unveiled his affordable, mass-produced Model T.

The computer industry saw a similar ramp up in the 1960s and 1970s. Competitive new companies like Digital Equipment Corporation emerged with low-price models that made computers affordable for places like retail stores and schools. At the same time, computer manufacturers had to make important engineering decisions. What was a better system for storing and transferring data? Punch cards? Magnetic tape? Those newfangled disk drives worked fast, but lost all your data when they failed. Market decisions were made, and prices dropped.

Neither the auto industry nor the computer industry enjoyed an easy transition. But it was far easier than what happened in the industries they replaced. The auto and computer industries were on the offensive, stealing new business and quickly expanding while old-style business lost customers and money.

Around 1900, manufacturers of traditional horse wagons felt compelled to defend their turf against the encroachment of the automobile. Such defensive posturing might have worked for a time. More efficient production and lower prices could make one company the best of a dying breed, bringing in a trickle of new business as other, less efficient horse wagon makers went out of business. But such a tactic usually makes it harder to transition to a new market space when the time eventually comes. **The lesson is: Don't spend time perfecting a dying art rather than making the leap to new business.** Better to realize that your current market space is transitioning. Better to aggressively stake out a position in the evolving new market space than rely on new income from a waning customer base.

In the computer industry, clerks, secretaries, managers of huge file archives, and those who handled billing for large businesses and small found their jobs suddenly changed with the arrival of the computer age. There was much moaning in the 1970s that computers were making people obsolete. But that didn't happen. Jobs became obsolete. But wise people acquired new skills that kept them employable as computers proliferated into nearly every industry.

All of this is just a precursor to what's happening as the computer age morphs into the Internet age. The fingers from this evolution, especially the e-commerce portion, reach so deep into the world's commercial landscape that an auto-industry-style shake-up looms for virtually all today's businesses.

The Future Belongs to the Assertive

Any new technology that significantly improves an existing business process usually spins off new markets and significantly affects existing markets and jobs. Workers follow the money. This process has been repeated over and over in history, from the rise of agriculture in ancient times, to the era of the tall ships, to the era of the railroad, steel mills, and beyond. Once a market is established, supply to and from that market becomes even more important. Every single part that goes into a manufactured product, every bit of data that leads to a decision, every single shred of media content that streams across a Web site, comes from some kind of a supplier, be it a live person or an automated process. Using the Internet to understand and control that supply chain is a vital function for a growing business. Yet most businesses don't even have a full picture of how all the supplies, facts, and so on arrive at their business and how they are all used, much less developed into a detailed supply chain strategy.

Consider this: Virtually no one who provides products these days can control every part of that product from raw material to finished good, nor handle everything from establishing a sales channel to implementing a marketing plan based on adequate research. Parts are bought preassembled. Functions are outsourced. Specialists are enlisted for limited projects. Companies focus on a few things and leave the rest to others. Anyone in business today needs to buy and rent products and services. And this creates ongoing supply and demand issues that need to be controlled.

The Internet makes it possible for any company to exchange information directly with any other company. It allows companies and customers to interact with one another, and for suppliers to actually target end users through the middle-tier companies they sell to.

E-mail is just a small part of this. Sharing data, inventory, invoices, pricing adjustments, shipping manifests, and so on are also part of the picture. Many companies are starting to connect their information systems to their partners, suppliers, and customers via customized extranets. Extranets allow participants to check inventory, place orders, and monitor the progress of those orders. If you serve an industry that's focusing on improving and controlling its supply chain (the auto industry is a leader in this), then you must be ready to participate in this process. The end goal—probably unattainable in its purest form, but certainly a target to shoot for—is for all functions of a business process to be done as a reaction to an order. A large enough extranet, with involvement from every point in your supply chain and your distribution system, should give you, in theory, enough data to completely perfect your business process, eliminating all waste.

How might this work? Let's say you want to order a new car online. In the radical new frontier of auto buying, the order is sent to the manufacturer, not a car dealer. The manufacturer immediately checks inventory, and first attempts to fill your order with an in-stock unit. (In theory, there should be no unsold stock at all, because everything is created on demand. But it's likely there will always be some premanufactured stock because of returns and order cancellations.)

If no stock is available, the order is echoed to all manufacturing units. The engine department needs to know to build an engine. The fenders, bumpers, and the interior must be constructed and moved to an assembly point. The vehicle is constructed, painted, and shipped.

The order is also propagated further back into the supply chain, so that the manufacturer's steel plant (whether it's owned or under contract) knows to produce just enough rolled steel to punch out the next set of fenders. In theory, the order should be propagated even further— all the way back to an iron mine, which needs to know that demand has ramped up even the tiniest fraction.

Today, that seems absurd. No one would ramp up a steel plant to produce a few sheets of steel. But with a better eye on downstream consumption, steel plants could be far different places. Instead of massive furnaces and football-field-sized mills and roller systems, operations might be more scalable with multiple smaller furnaces. This is more expensive when all furnaces are firing, but cheaper when the operation scales up and down with demand. Also, with a heavily automated, scalable set of smaller furnaces, the steel plants could be in multiple locations, improving the distribution system.

This is beyond the so-called just-in-time manufacturing process that received a lot of promotion in the late 1990s. This is really market-pull, reactionary manufacturing that includes a just-in-time element because partner data is widely known. The better you can implement such a system, the closer you can get to making only what you need to make, reducing waste and storage costs. You won't tie up capital unnecessarily. You'll reduce shipping and storage costs and push other costs onto your partners. Plus, engineers will be able to change designs quickly because they won't have a warehouse of parts to use up first.

This level of supply change management would never be possible without the Internet. It's the chief reason that interest in supply chain management as a cost-cutting measure has grown right along with the Net. Just look at the two-year stock chart for application software companies that focus on supply chain and enterprise resource planning (ERP). Siebel Systems, I2, and Veritas Software all show fantastic growth that mirrors manufacturers' interest in their products and services.

Getting a God's-eye view of supply and demand via data from your partners creates measurable value within the B2B evolution. The idea has manufacturers, suppliers, and Internet services providers around the world watching key solutions and marketplace builders like CommerceOne and supply chain applications builders (the ERP stalwarts listed previously), plus database powerhouses like Oracle. And the world wonders, which of these evolving powerhouses will win the larger share of the new supply chain management pie? If the evolution continues, could one of them become the next Microsoft? (Microsoft has played some in this space too, via its value chain initiative and enterprise systems group. So the next Microsoft could very well be . . . Microsoft.)

The fly in the ointment here is that, to get that God's-eye view, data must be accurate. But will the people you buy from and the people you sell to provide the data you need? Not in today's world. Maybe your supplier has inventory. But it wants to sell that inventory to your chief competitor. The easy answer from them is nothing's available. Today, you have to take their word for it; it's unlikely you could change that. And do you want others to know you have a warehouse full of merchandise and no demand for your product? If they did, they'd pressure you for a better price.

Systems like this only work in an open world where most things are treated as commodities with prices that fluctuate like a stock market. That's starting to happen. Most buyers today look to the Net for pricing and new suppliers. Thus, people who can build massive exchanges for specialized goods and services have a fair chance of constructing the important next phase of the Internet.

The marketplace concept is also catching on in other industries. Seven of the world's largest investment banks, including The Goldman Sachs Group, Merrill Lynch, Morgan Stanley Dean Witter, Salomon Smith Barney, and Credit Suisse First Boston, worked together to create TheMarkets.com, a portal for institutional investors. It offers equity research, new issue information, news, and market data, as well as easy direct access to the subscription Web sites of the participants.

Right now, we don't see many shoppers purchasing cars online. But many consumers do use the Web to conduct research on the brands they want. Moving these shoppers toward online buying will stoke the beginnings of the consumer-pull/supply chain prediction process that will surpass JIT manufacturing. A Goldman Sachs report predicted that

---

For a fascinating overview on how the product development and deployment cycle works, visit the massive Internet trade exchange called Covisint that's being developed by Ford Motor Company, Daimler-Chrysler AG, General Motors Corporation, and Renault/Nissan. The interesting thing is how the organization's public face is constructed at www.covisint.com. Before signing up to participate in the trade center, you can read a great deal about the group's theories on how procurement cycles work, and how product development feeds into it. There's even a large section on how supply chains are built and a self-centered view of how Net-based solutions like Covisint work.

There is no denying that trade exchanges like this one will have a huge impact, because of the big names and market muscle behind the effort. Suppliers who want to remain suppliers are forced to plug in and participate.

---

cost savings could reach $3,000 per auto for a system that takes advantage of all this information and properly controls product supply and parts purchasing.

Now let's extrapolate this trend. What if all functions in the auto manufacturing process are outsourced to the most efficient supplier, including services like design, assembly, and distribution? Auto companies could simply become brand managers rather than manufacturers who hold weighty investments in things like auto plants and high-maintenance machinery. Meanwhile, the Internet brings them closer to their customers and offers a venue for selling, delivering, and servicing new vehicles.

The transition to pure brand management will happen, if not by leading automakers, then by aggressive upstarts. It's usually the innovators with a financial interest in new processes or technologies that initiate a market transition. It wasn't the wagon makers who started the move toward horseless carriages. Benz was not a wagon maker. He made engines and looked to create new markets for his product.

Likewise, in the early days of the Internet, you didn't see established retailers like Wal-Mart or Sears rushing to develop online commerce. They already had a successful retail model. Online commerce was a pipe dream. The Internet retail market sector was necessarily created by upstart retailers looking for a market niche and upstart computer makers and software companies looking for new business. It was high risk and rich reward for those who pulled it off. This focus on exploiting new technologies is what allowed companies like Amazon.com to carve out new business in a space that didn't previously exist.

Another parallel between the auto industry and the Internet industry is how the transition evolved. Not everyone changed to autos immediately because the technology was expensive, immature, and unreliable at first (sound familiar?). Plus, there wasn't a decent infrastructure of smooth roads and gas stations. Occasional cars may have been spotted on roads in the last 20 years of the nineteenth century, but the auto market didn't reach critical mass until around 1910. That's why wagon makers like F. Ronstadt of Tucson were able to do a fine business despite the appearance of cars, then slowly morph into an auto dealership. That's why dial-up lines still exist in the era of digital subscriber lines and why snailmail and e-mail orders are still popular in the era of online transaction processing.

But wagon makers, horse traders, and blacksmith shops slowly felt the squeeze created by the shift to a new transportation paradigm. They had a lot of warning that the shift was coming. Many found new jobs within the new infrastructure, helping to build roads, build cars, or even pump gas. Those who didn't make the switch saw their prospects dim. They were eventually forced to make a transition anyway, but not from a position of strength.

The same is true for the shifting retail landscape. Today, traditional retailers continue to thrive. But as they move online, their online presence seems to be breaking into different market segments.

1. **Huge national chains will continue to operate their megastores, but their online presence will become a growing part of their business.** The sheer volume of their sales will give them a price advantage that will be hard to compete against, for both online and offline vendors. This means so-called old economy retailers, though they came late to the game, are becoming a powerful online retail presence anyway because of the capital, branding, and distribution they've brought to the table.

Wal-Mart and Sears didn't ride the first wave of online retailing. They joined the game once they acknowledged the powerful transition. That's typical for market leaders. IBM didn't jump into the personal computer fray quickly. It let the new guys fight it out. It watched to see which technologies proved themselves and which companies emerged victorious. IBM eventually aligned itself with the Microsoft Disk Operating System (MS-DOS) and joined the PC revolution. It arrived late, but brought the muscle to dictate the next phase of the revolution. Huge national retailers like Wal-Mart are in a position to dictate terms to suppliers. Anyone who sells products to Wal-Mart has to follow a specific model and use Wal-Mart's own software. Wal-Mart might eventually set certain standards for the e-commerce retail sector, such as how online transactions are channeled through a payment system, and who ships ordered products.

2. **Some regional stores may not need to transition to online e-commerce. Their advantage is proximity and convenience, not price and selection.** A simple Web page advertising their wares and offering directions to their store may be enough. They may want to dabble in online sales, but if they deal in commodity items, it's unlikely the Web will create an avalanche of new business for them. Your local newsstand will continue to sell papers and magazines to meet your immediate needs, but you're probably not going to order a magazine online from them. If you're willing to wait a few days for shipping, you'll likely order from the Web site that gives you the best price.

One exception is when there are variations in regional inventory, such as at car dealers. A customer who wants that green Sebring convertible with the tan roof and leather interior may not find one at the dealer down the street. But he would certainly want to know if that very car is available just 20 miles away. Thus, car dealers have made good use of the Web. So have real-estate agents.

But it's unreasonable to expect a potential customer to browse 20 local Web sites to find just the right car. Local dealers found a more efficient way of reaching potential buyers in their region. To extend their reach, many dealers participate in online marketing alliances and comparison shopping services like Autoweb.com, Autobytel.com, and CarsDirect.com. Involvement in these systems, rather than trying to extend their reach through a single Web site, helps regional dealers gain better distribution of their product listings. It also makes proximity nearly as important as price point.

Another exception to the rule is specialized delivery services like Urbanfetch.com. With offices in London and New York City, Urbanfetch is basically a convenience store. Its gig is free delivery anywhere in the city, often in under an hour. When delivery is part of the mix, local stores can easily compete via the Net. But such an effort needs to be tightly focused. Urbanfetch eventually migrated away from consumer service to concentrate on business supplies sold to a tight downtown core.

3. **Specialty stores have an advantage in online commerce. They offer something that's hard to find.** Their customers are scattered all over the map, and they specifically use the Web to research and find specialty items. Today there are still businesses that manufacture horse wagons, blacksmith-style wrought iron, buggy whips, and horse tack. You can't walk into Sears or even your local feed store to buy a wagon wheel anymore. But you can purchase them online from specialty shops.

Stop by any antique auto show and ask the car owners if their hobby has been made easier on the Web. You'll probably find someone who searched in vain for years for a replacement tail light for a 1947 Ford. Then they finally found it on an antique auto parts Web site.

Specialty stores, wherever they are located, have a great reason to move into online product catalogs and e-commerce. It's their prime way of finding new customers because the customers are already using the Web trying to find them.

Strangely enough, it was the pornography industry that pioneered the online specialty store niche and stimulated the e-commerce industry. They were some of the first small businesses to accept credit cards online, and to arrange quick shipping of products or quick access to pictures by autoprocessing card numbers. Suddenly everyone from the backwoods of Maine to the beaches of Baja had access to adult content they couldn't find, or didn't want to buy, locally. The model was quickly replicated by such businesses as gardening stores selling seeds, and bookstores, and quilting supply shops.

Because each market segment has different models and tactics, retailers must decide which market segment they're targeting—national presence with volume discounts, regional presence with service and convenience, or a specialty emporium working to establish a broader reach. Moving online without clearly identifying your target market is a mistake.

One other way today's tech industry parallels the auto industry is in the inevitability of consolidation. Since the 1880s, nearly 1,000 companies have produced finished automobiles in the United States. (And in this case, being first mover in the industry didn't make a difference. How many of us ever heard of Duryea, supposedly the first U.S.-produced car?)

Some of these fledgling car manufacturers went out of business. But most never really disappeared. They sold assets to each other. They merged and merged again. For example, in 1954 two very famous names in the auto industry, Hudson and Nash, merged to create American Motors. That was their way of dealing with the growing dominance of General Motors and the long-term market muscle of Ford Motor Company.

By 1970, American Motors also purchased the popular Jeep line of four-wheel-drive vehicles from Kaiser Corporation. Kaiser had previously picked up the Jeep products from Willys Overland in the early 1950s. In 1987, Chrysler purchased AMC, whittling the top four U.S. automakers down to the Big Three. By the late 1990s, global consolidation made its presence known when the German powerhouse Daimler-Benz merged with Chrysler to form DaimlerChrysler. (This proves just how different business combat is from real-world combat. Through mergers and acquisitions, not shooting and bombing, a German company became the owner of Jeep, one of the weapons that helped the Allies defeat Germany in World War II.)

This is the sort of consolidation we are seeing in the Internet today. Yet, there are still thousands of highly popular .com sites. The consolidation will continue for years.

There are other examples of huge consolidations in other industries. As demand for electric lighting grew in the late 1800s, small coal and hydroelectric power plants appeared in many towns and cities. Eventually, large regional companies consolidated from these smaller services, and the tiny plants were replaced. Small-town department stores and lumberyards were either purchased or put out of business by encroaching chain and mall stores. Guess who absorbed the workers, the customers, and sometimes the buildings from those older businesses?

Consolidation is an indication of maturity in an industry. The move toward that maturity is most apparent in the large .com companies themselves. To gain page views and market reach, Yahoo purchased the popular Web-page-hosting service known as GeoCities. Lycos purchased the high-tech search engine HotBot and the Web-page-hosting services Tripod and Angelfire. @Home merged with Excite. Meanwhile, Internet service providers experienced their own consolidation frenzy, with giants like NetCom merging with EarthLink. The early consolidators are building the media monoliths of the next 20 years.

Surprisingly, the trend toward consolidation is not universal. Sometimes, a mature, established market can suddenly expand once again, causing new companies and product offerings to skyrocket, leading to new fragmentation of an industry. That's what happened to the television industry in the 1980s. Cable TV was the catalyst. After lurking in some remote regions of the country since the 1950s, cable television exploded in the 1980s, bringing hundreds of channels to middle America.

ABC, CBS, and NBC never regained the total market share they enjoyed in the 1960s and 1970s. We did see consolidation of a type— a few owners of cable TV systems became dominant throughout the country. But outside of the cable systems themselves, thousands of content providers emerged. No small handful of key providers was ever able to totally dominate the industry again, though Turner and Viacom have certainly tried. In time, dominant content providers may emerge.

The Courage of Your Convictions

At times like these, when everyone around you is losing their heads, it is time for long-range plans and bold moves. That's why this chapter is about developing your offensive strategy, which includes both a tech strategy and aggressive product development and distribution plans. Yes, developing a long-range posture is difficult to do. You don't know which technology will be a huge winner one year from now, much less five years out. You don't know how markets will shift. You could make the wrong decision, and lose the game.

Make the plans anyway. You likely will not hit a moving target. You definitely won't hit it if you don't shoot for it. You don't have to bet everything. Just bet enough to still be in the game if you win or lose. Just like wagon maker Ronstadt, who slowly shifted to auto sales, you can adapt into a new technology just enough to establish a foothold and create a revenue stream. Blend the revenue stream with your other business. The market will eventually tell you if you have a winner. You will have made the right offensive move if it is. A good example is how music companies reacted to the music file-sharing system, Napster—by lawsuit. Finally, they saw Beitelsman's BMG Entertainment and others embrace Napster as they fought to embrace the new medium and combat the digital rights management issues.

Internet consulting companies are another good example of businesses with differing strategies for preparing for the future. They are specialists that help other businesses design and develop their Web or e-commerce strategies. Some of these consultants grew out of traditional computer industries like systems integrators or database administrators. Some were raw start-ups that claim pure Internet status, handling nothing but Net sites and e-commerce from day one. Still others are offshoots of large consulting companies like PricewaterhouseCoopers, which built an information technology service so large it ended up trying to sell the entire division to Hewlett-Packard before that deal imploded.

In 1999, Internet consulting companies saw their stock prices rise at unprecedented levels. Slick and talented companies like Viant, Razorfish, iXL Enterprises, and Sapient seemed to rule the world. Everyone needed their services. Everyone thought they were cool, especially Razorfish, which seemed to drip attitude and attracted both media companies (from *Cosmopolitan* magazine to NBC) and investment sites like Charles Schwab.

These consultants don't design simple Web sites with HTML pages. They design high-end, graphically rich systems with dynamic pages built from databases. They help integrate secure e-commerce systems with minimal downtime. They make catalogs that can be updated in real time. That's exactly what media companies and retailers moving to the Web in the 1990s needed. Business was great.

So here is how it all played out. Viant stock rose from 20 to 60 between September and mid-December 1999. IXL rocketed from the mid-20s to 55. Razorfish's wild ride took it from 15 to about 56, and Sapient jumped from 20 to 75. And after the April 2000 NASDAQ plunge? Viant fell back to 20, Razorfish pulled all the way back to about 16, iXL crept down into the teens, and Sapient landed in the 30s.

The sheen was off Wall Street's Web darlings. By fall 2000, some of those losses were regained, but analyst ratings, with a series of up-grades and downgrades, kept the stock prices bouncing. Viant fell all the way to the single digits by September 2000.

The value of these companies was bid into the stratosphere because it seemed like they had an endless supply of business. Major companies were willing to pay them big bucks. Those who bought stock in these and other Internet companies were not investing in the next quarter's profit. They were buying into the future growth of proven winners.

The April 2000 NASDAQ plunge showed a change in the industry trend. Demand for development projects was slowing. Increasingly, as businesses shopped for price, they slowed their adaptation of new fea-tures and functions. Once their slick front pages and databases were in place, some buyers started looking to traditional outsourcers and con-sulting firms for future contracts. The once cutting-edge consultant firms found their services had become a commodity.

Once the rapid growth of any market slows, it becomes more dan-gerous to bet strictly on future growth. At that point, fast-rising com-panies have to start playing by traditional rules, like showing a profit and developing powerful partnerships.

Basically, the market changed 180 degrees in one year for pure Internet companies. Not only did growth slow, but the threat of encroachment appeared, not from below (smaller, hungrier companies) but from above (powerful business service and consulting companies such as KPMG International, Arthur Andersen, and PricewaterhouseCoopers). These knowledgeable business stalwarts had developed their own e-commerce consulting units and started aiming squarely at Fortune 500 companies who might not trust their business to talented but attitude-heavy upstarts. They siphoned some of the highest value customers.

This prompted many analytical articles like the one at the CBS MarketWatch Web site that asked, "What's Your .com Exposure?" It indicated that the Web consulting pullback and brutal industry consolidation were indicative of the shape of things to come. It said the pullback would affect money invested in .com companies. It would bleed over into other sectors, like site hosting, application development, and Internet access services. Other analysts warned of great risk and tremendous loss for any investor strictly still playing the growth game for Internet stocks.

The exception was infrastructure. The feeling remains that there are only a handful of key players providing the fiber optics, routers, and the networking equipment used to construct the ever-expanding Internet. So these companies will thrive. Companies like Cisco and even Corning (because of its glass-based optical cable products) did very well in 2000.

All this should have indicated that the time was right, in the fall of 2000, for .com companies to either cash out or hunker down with a wait-and-see attitude. Logic might dictate that they work to satisfy current customers, and watch to see how consolidation shook out other players. Maybe they could pick up pieces from those other businesses.

Many did take that approach. But they are not likely to be the key leaders for the next 10 years.

Winners are those who gamble a bit. Not to risk all, but just to get out ahead of the curve to see where things are going. If you have the right product, are partnered with the right people and focused on the best emerging technology, you will be better established as the consolidation slows and winners emerge. That's an important point. On the Net, there is no quiet time. Get out. Anticipate. Conquer. Adjust your business plan as often as necessary and go after that moving target.

Of course, the age-old question is, How do you know? How do you know what the winning technology will be? How do you know which companies to partner with? How do you know you're building a killer application that will keep you in business? The answer is, You don't. But other people do. The market knows who the winners will be, and that's where you pick up your clues. As a market matures, winners slowly emerge, not overnight as they sometimes do in a hot new market. You see the winners and the contenders in the trade magazine stories. You see them at conferences. Find out who your competitors are talking about and working with. Ask them why. Make your adjustments as the winds shift. Don't fall asleep and miss those winds of change. And don't ignore the winds because you're sure your way is best. Even if you do have the best system and the best technology, so what? Many people said Betamax was a better video system than VHS, but the market declared VHS the winner instead. Those who bet on VHS won big.

Pay attention. Look for the opening. Look to make the big play. That's what it means to play offense.

You've heard this saying your whole life: "The best defense is a good offense." Here's the logic behind the cliché. If all you do is defend, you become worn down and will never advance. If you want to protect your interests, often you actually have to expand and control that which is important to you.

Most generals, including Sun Tzu, realize this to be true. If your company got to the Internet early and grabbed a chunk of valuable real estate and a good user base, you need to maintain that offensive posture during the consolidation phase. You're not just looking to protect your stake, you're looking to pick up new products and new market reach as others drop out.

Likewise, if you've been standing back, waiting for the market to develop so you can see where to concentrate your next efforts, it's still time to go on the offensive, to purchase an established business at a good price to gain customers and revenue. Or maybe it's time to start a new product development effort to target some underserved niche you've noticed while standing back. The trick is to stay focused on expansion, even as others shrink. It will help you learn how to react and prepare for the next shift.

Leveraging current assets can give you a quick start. Bob Bickel, executive VP of products at Bluestone software, which was acquired by Hewlett-Packard in February 2001, told me of an internal resource at *Time* magazine that became an external e-commerce application, via a developer using Bluestone tools.

Time magazine's internal picture collection contains 20 million photos, stored in a New York City basement. Advertisers could order images, but staffers had to search out requests. They built an intranet so people who took the photo calls from ad agencies could look it up to see if they had anything, according to Bickel. They soon realized they had a great asset and opened it up to the public. At www.thepicturecollection.com, you can search for anything, and see a watermarked low-resolution photo or buy a high-resolution version.

In his book *The Road Ahead,* Bill Gates says, "Success is a lousy teacher. It seduces smart people into thinking they can't lose." In a rapidly changing economy, he says, a perfect business plan doesn't stay perfect because it goes out of date quickly. Gates also says, "You can't count on conventional wisdom. That only makes sense in conventional markets."

The Internet, in its rapid expansion phase (which isn't over) and its remarkable consolidation phase (which is ongoing), is definitely not a conventional market. Because of rapidly changing technology, and because some companies fail to account for these changes, companies that were very large 20 years ago have disappeared, while others have grown from nothing to billions of dollars in value in a short period of time. For example, Lycos went from a concept in a university lab to a successful $9 billion company in about five years at its top market cap. Yahoo took about six years to become a $60 billion company at its peak. These were great offense plays because they were executed at just the right time. The Net was young. People didn't even realize they needed directories and search services to navigate. But when they did, some smart people had already anticipated their needs.

Roll Out the Big Guns? Or Will Pea Shooters Do?

But how great an offense should you mount? A scorched-earth policy, wherein companies are purchased and liquidated, may add to your bottom line. But failure looms.

In the modern world, a surprisingly large amount of business is built through cooperation and joint agreement. Think of it as the chamber of commerce approach to expanding everyone's business horizons to keep the whole town happy. This may differ from the Saddam Hussein school of warfare where you try to outmuscle everyone and burn everything to the ground. But the chamber of commerce approach is actually in keeping with Sun Tzu's philosophy. He always allowed an enemy a way out. And he'd rather work with a strong ally than fight a tough competitor.

If you're the scorched-earth type, you may gain market share, but you lose something in the process. The cost is great on your own people—the people who have to do the dirty deeds. It's hard enough to find worker loyalty these days.

Focus on loyalty. Workers are unlikely to feel loyal to a company that liquidates others with little thought or worry for those employees. Also, when you pick up a competing brand, it will have its own loyal customers. If you disappoint those customers, you will not maintain their loyalty. The company you purchase will lose some of its value, reducing your return on investment.

115

Thus, compassion in business, and understanding the needs and motivations of your competition, remain important. Yet it's more complex than that. Even if you don't intend to acquire a competitor, it may be better not to drive the company into the ground. There are two reasons for this.

1. Sometimes having more than one operation serving a market niche keeps the niche viable in the mind of the public. Advertisers, suppliers, and customers are all attracted to a dynamic market with more than one vendor. A single controlling company that serves a market niche doesn't create a dynamic market. It looks less interesting. It receives less attention and sometimes less money.

2. Your opponent may fight harder than you think if survival of its business is at stake. Sun Tzu proposed that it's better not to destroy your enemy, but to let the enemy live. You are actually more likely to win a war if the enemy is not faced with fighting to the death. If you can give them an out, they are more likely to take that escape if they think they could not win anyway. It is easier on both the winner and the loser, and it's the logical choice for both.

What might such an escape be? Perhaps it is concentration on a secondary market or a distribution channel of less use to you. Think of the cola wars. Regional soda pop manufacturers are happy selling their product through mom-and-pop shops while Coke and Pepsi control the supermarkets and major vending machine locations.

If a company's owners and employees have invested great time and wealth in their venture, they will not want to let it die. Confronting them head-on with the intention of stealing all their business will backfire. They will do whatever is necessary to survive, including working long hours, charging lower prices, slashing staff and costs, and bidding low to provide a greater value to their customers to win back market share.

For example, a Forrester study of e-marketplaces found several serious businesses that claimed they didn't want advertising as part of their online marketplaces. Yet by the summer of 2000, these businesses were calling ad services bureaus to implement this additional revenue stream. Some moved to participate in group ad services, even though that might mean working with their competition.

Better to think strategically than combatively. Your first strategy should never be openly combative, even if heavy confrontation is eventually necessary. If it is, make sure the battle is fought with a clear strategic objective, which can include pushing the opponent in a certain direction. Used effectively, you can push them out of your market space, allowing them to live on, but not as your rival.

Most people don't know that electronics giant Nintendo was in the playing card business 100 years ago. By the 1950s, competition in that industry pushed Nintendo in other directions, first marketing novelty cards with licensed Disney and other cartoon characters, and then developing and selling games, which eventually became their core business. In the 1970s, they started adding electronic elements to games, making them ready for the computer revolution in gaming.

In retrospect, the company didn't really take off until it faced difficulty expanding within the traditional card market. Because Nintendo found a lucrative out by moving to novelty cards and games, other card manufacturers picked up business with minimal competition, and the move was definitely a winning situation in the long run for Nintendo.

If one of those other card companies had purchased Nintendo instead, and kept its wise workers and managers in place and focused on strategic expansion, imagine where it would be today.

When outright competition is necessary, Sun Tzu says, "Generally, in war the best policy is to take a state intact; to ruin it is inferior to this. To capture the enemy's entire army is better than to destroy it; to take intact a regiment, a company, or a squad is better than to destroy them. For to win one hundred victories in one hundred bat-

tles is not the pinnacle of skill. To subdue the enemy without fighting
is the supreme authority."

So, if you and an opponent desire to control the same market
space, does this mean you should work toward a merger rather than
fighting? That depends entirely on the opponent and your view of their
abilities. What is your business model? What is theirs? What is the
price of their goods and their ability to deliver to key customers? Do
you have the exact same pieces of the puzzle? Or does one of you have
a better production system and the other a better distribution system?
What are the asking price and the merger terms? Who would control
the combined company? If you are a public company, would a merger
help or hurt your share price?

If the answers to these questions are unsatisfactory, or if the combined company would not have better synergy, then fighting it out may
be better than a merger. But the intense, damaging competition should
be a last resort. You may end up like gas stations across the street from
each other engaged in an intense price war. Both sides incur damage by
sacrificing everything they can to offer the lower price. Working for a
win-win situation is best, but only if you can indeed succeed through
such cooperation.

If you realize you must fight, move swiftly, and have a plan that
includes both your long-term strategy and ways you will answer any
challenges. To defeat your opponent, you must anticipate and devastate
the opponent's strategy. You need to know their motives and their business process.

This is a hazy, complicated formula, and it's more complicated on
the Internet than in the physical world where you know where the
opponents' factories are located, and when their products ship. When
companies compete for business via the Internet, there are thousands
of ways to proceed, and you can't monitor every move or notice every
transaction.

Here's what you *can* watch: Perhaps your competition sells products via online catalogs. Or maybe they use auctions, third-party distributors, or package deals. You can use the Net to monitor this, check prices, and get an idea of targeted markets. You can set up a temporary e-mail account at one of several free mail services like Yahoo Mail, Lycos Mail, or Microsoft's Hotmail.com. From there, you can pose as a potential customer, sending an e-mail query to their sales offices. How long does it take them to respond? Do they route you through a national or a regional sales office? Can they answer your questions? Is their information accurate? Can they quote prices? Do they operate an e-mail list that you can sign up for? This information helps you learn about their operations. Likewise, they can learn about yours.

Here's what's difficult to watch: Your competition may be building limited online partnerships and distribution methods that will be hard to see. Perhaps they've arranged a complicated series of banner ads and special placement deals on other people's Web sites. That could give them access to new markets that you didn't know about. (Hint—if you see third-party ads or products highlighted on your competitor's Web site, visit that third party's Web site, too. You may discover that your competitor's products are also featured there.)

Your competition may also outsource parts of its order-taking or delivery systems to telesales contractors or fulfillment houses. In fact, so many things can be outsourced on the Web, it may never be possible to get a clear picture of your foe's costs or business model.

The safe way to fight uncertainty is to assume the worst, and plan accordingly. Thus, even if you have the money for big ad campaigns and target marketing, you still are forced to also use the same guerrilla marketing tactics and organic growth processes as your lowest-margin competitor. Some examples: If you are a service provider, you can use strategic partnerships for cross-promotion, and these can be as effective as expensive magazine ads. Perhaps no money changes hands. Perhaps you both charge the other for services and include the exchange in your P&L

statements. Maybe you include each other's logos on your advertising. Perhaps you drop each other's brochures into boxes before shipping.

If you are a media company, you can find ways to let your customers build content for you that you then repackage and sell. Think of the huge Web-hosting services like GeoCities and Tripod. They provide Web site–building tools and offer free Web-hosting services. Visitors then build Web pages to promote anything from small businesses to special interests and hobbies. The host sites create directories and search services to help other visitors find what they want. The hosts gain page views and advertising income from other people's content. A similar approach is found in the clubs sections of Yahoo, Lycos, or Excite. Visitors can create their own club based on a specific theme. Other visitors can join the club and leave messages, photos, and files. Each club has a specific chat area, where visitors can find each other. At a certain point, the concept jells and page views skyrocket. People visit the site to view club content, and eventually join the club, becoming repeat visitors and additional content providers.

The Internet offers literally millions of options for gathering, arranging, and influencing the flow of information and its presentation. The context behind how information is shared continues to be a driving force for successful Web ventures.

Yet when a clear context for information exchange emerges out of the noise of an online marketplace, a corresponding clear business strategy must also emerge. Just as important, you must seek out and recognize your opponent's strategy, hoping that you'll also be able to recognize their online business plan in the process.

In modern business, what you attack is not the enemy, but the enemy's strategy.

• Learn it, then disrupt it. Once you identify what the strategy is, you can disrupt alliances. Your opponent has partnerships. Your opponent belongs to organizations and industry groups. Your opponent has signed on to participate with certain standards and practices. If you can disrupt these, you can affect the opponent's power and abilities.

• Learn it and improve on it. Once you identify your opponent's strategies, you can improve on them, and then lure away customers. Can you find a cheaper distribution method? Micro Warehouse, a huge distributor of computers, electronics, networking, and other equipment, found success in the early 1990s by locating its distribution center near an airport. It could give boxes to an overnight delivery carrier at the last minute, shaving a day off the delivery time of afternoon orders. It also focused on price, and was able to undercut computer store chains by not having the costly overhead of leased store space, not to mention the challenges of stocking inventory at multiple locations.

• Learn it and absorb it. Once you identify your opponent's strategies, you can learn if what they do complements your operation. You may decide it's best to talk with them about a merger, offering an arrangement from which you both could benefit. Or maybe you only want to absorb specific workers or technologies.

• Learn it and change it. Knowing your opponent's strategies can help you stall or discredit their work. By knowing their interests, perhaps you can get them involved in side projects that will be unprofitable while you concentrate on the emerging business that will be profitable—allowing you to control that new, emerging space.

• Learn it and destroy it. The last choice is to take on the company, full force, attacking its main market space. This is the most work for you, and the greatest threat to them. The threat will not be ignored, and it may turn out to be your hardest and least-effective option.

Sun Tzu says, "The worst policy is to attack cities. Attack cities only when there is no alternative because to prepare big shields and wagons and make ready the necessary arms and equipment requires at least three months, and to pile up earthen ramps against the walls requires an additional three months. The general, unable to control his impatience, will order his troops to swarm up the wall like ants, with the result that one-third of them will be killed without taking the city. Such is the calamity of attacking cities."

To preserve capital, time, and energy, the greatest skill a leader can have is to subdue the opponent without a major struggle. This is the true art of offensive strategy—not so much fighting, as outsmarting. Advance slowly and methodically so that your own workers, in fact all your resources, are not worn down and dissatisfied. Advance so that you take what you want before others even know it's available, and give them an out.

With such a plan, you will be well positioned and well rested for those times when you must meet an opponent head-on. When that does happen, here are some rules of thumb.

- When you greatly outnumber the opponent, when you have more business, more partners, and more resources, surround him and work harder than he does. He will not be able to keep up.

- When you slightly outnumber the opponent, attack and push the opponent back, or try to divide that organization against itself, so that the opponent is not clear on his own strategy.

- If you and your opponent are equally matched, resource-wise, you may engage her if you are confident that you have a good plan. But a joint venture or a merger may work just as well if you bring different talents to the mix.

- If you are weaker numerically, or undercapitalized, strike where the opponent is vulnerable, not where he is strongest. And be capable of withdrawing or shifting to a moderately different direction, should your challenge be answered.

- If you are smaller than your opponent, if you have fewer resources and a big task ahead of you, be capable of eluding the opponent for any sort of head-on challenge. A small business is something a larger business feeds on, taking workers and stealing your business and your market share. In such a case, you cannot deal with your opponent recklessly.

Sun Tzu says, "The general is the assistant to the sovereign of the state. If this assistance is all-embracing, the state will surely be strong; if defective, the state will certainly be weak."

Likewise, the CEO is the assistant to the board of directors and, in many ways, the champion of his employees. The CEO is the general that gives the organization its strength, purpose, and marching orders. His or her judgment must be sound.

The threat against the state is different than the threat against a corporation. People will not die if a business falls. Social systems will not collapse. Fortunes may crumble, but not for everyone. Workers will find work elsewhere. CEOs will get hired again. Assets can be sold off, possibly at a profit. It's unlikely anyone will be executed. Business carries many of the benefits of real war, with few of the nasty side effects. Thus an aggressive business strategy is more fun and less risky.

Yet there are distinct patterns that emerge in both war and business. When Sun Tzu talks about how sovereigns sometimes don't understand the work of an army, he could certainly be talking about boards of directors or stockholders who don't understand the strategy of the CEO. If you have faith in a CEO, the CEO must be allowed to make decisions affecting day-to-day operations.

• Just as an army faces a disadvantage if a ruler orders an attack before the troops are prepared, so too is an organization hobbled and weakened when the board of directors orders the team to advance into some new project or business area when they are not ready. This is often done when a new market space is emerging, but the workers are already pushed to the breaking point. A similar situation is when the company is asked to retreat and give up a portion of a market space, when they are poised to claim and control that space. It should be the CEO's job to gauge the timing of such operations and their profitability. The CEO is closest to the front lines.

- **When ignorant of business affairs as they apply to a particular competitive or technology-focused market, decisions about this market should be left to the experts the company has hired.** When directors or stockholders interfere in the affairs of a highly technical product, management becomes perplexed and confidence in the organization's direction wanes. The whole operation risks looking like a giant Dilbert cartoon.

- **When ignorant of organizational and logistical problems that management faces, interference with product development or marketing creates doubts in the minds of workers and middle management.** Sometimes confidence in a leader is more important for winning than knowing that the battle could have been won faster if the leader took, say, the east path around the mountain rather than the west. Leaders will sometimes make mistakes. But micromanagement of the leader's decisions from well-intentioned outsiders may thwart the leader from ever fully engaging in the battle he or she is destined to win.

These situations cause confusion, suspicion, and waning motivation in an organization. Competitors will notice the chaos and take advantage of this, luring workers, delaying projects, and depressing stock prices.

Sun Tzu says, "A confused army leads to another's victory."

To win, avoid confusion. Make sure the organization's goals are known, and that the CEO is the one responsible for calling the plays and attaining goals. Here are five points in which victory may be predicted.

1. **Both the CEO and board of directors must know when the company can rise to a challenge and win and when it cannot. Only with this knowledge can the company be victorious.**

2. **The CEO who understands how to fight in accordance with the strengths, weaknesses, and strategy of the opponent will be vic-**

torious. The CEO must also know the strengths and weaknesses of his or her own company. (Self-appraisal and appraising your opponent are outlined in Chapter 1.)

3. The company's ranks must be united in purpose, with clear goals and proper timelines. Scattered efforts and ego-draining side projects waste energy.

4. The organization must be well prepared and lie in wait to take advantage of unprepared and unorganized opponents.

5. The company's CEO and upper management are able and qualified, and are not interfered with by any uninformed persons.

If these five issues are installed, even a smaller organization challenging a larger, established opponent has a great chance for success.

A smaller, nimbler organization is better in some areas particularly suited for rapidly evolving new e-business opportunities. Like a smaller boxer going up against a bigger opponent, confidence, timing, and accuracy become more important than brute force.

It is very important, as you plan your offense, to apply the lessons in Chapter 1.

• If you know your opponent and yourself, you will plan your offense correctly. You will never be defeated because you know the right time to enter battle and the right moves to make as you engage.

• If you know yourself, but are ignorant of your opponent, your chances of winning or losing are equal. You can make great plans, but they may be the wrong plans based on your specific opponent. You may find yourself changing too much, too late in the confrontation.

• If ignorant of both your opponent and yourself, you are sure to be defeated in every battle. Your products may not find buyers. Market share will be lost. Your organization will shrink.

TOOLS YOU CAN USE

Here are some tools you can use to gain the edge over competitors.

The Gartner Group

- It offers detailed industry analysis and market research. It also generates general reports or customized analysis and planning. Heavy emphasis is on information infrastructure.

- One of the largest collections of analysts in the industry, with a network of 35,000 clients.

- Web site: www.gartner.com

- Slogan: "Insight for the connected world."

Jupiter Media Metrix

- Jupiter is the research and advisory service branch. It offers qualitative and quantitative analysis with an emphasis on Internet marketing.

- Web site: www.jup.com

- Media Metrix is a part of Jupiter that offers audience and e-commerce measurement services and rankings of Web sites based on Internet traffic. The detailed reports are a great way to see how you stack up to your competition for raw page views. It's also a way to keep an eye on new market movers.

- Web site: www.mediametrix.com/

- Jupiter slogan: "The world wide authority on Internet commerce."

- Media Metrix slogan: "Source: Media Metrix."

Forrester Research

- The focus is strategic research for market positioning and technographics measuring attitudes and behavior of Internet users. Provides online assessment tools for markets.

- Web site: www.forrester.com

- Slogan: "Helping business thrive on technology change."

New Technology or Business Partner Discovery

- Ariba, IBM, and Microsoft are developing a way for companies to participate in virtual online marketplaces by listing descriptions of their businesses and e-commerce systems in a central directory. The system is called Universal Description, Discovery, and Integration (UDDI). Several supply chain system developers have signed on to the project. (www.uddi.com)

- Hoover's Online is a great place to do research on a company to learn what they make, what their market is, and how successful they are. "Business Boneyard" is an interesting read, but not a spot to find successful competitors. (www.hoovers.com)

- Red Herring Online—this magazine tracks venture capital and who's doing what in high-tech business. Here you can find research into new technologies and their impact on industry. (www.redherring .com)

- Manufacturing Marketplace—trade journals and suppliers directories. (www.manufacturingmarketplace.com)

- The New Media Lab at the Massachusetts Institute of Technology offers insight and community for those interested in cutting-edge computer technologies. (www.media.mit.edu/)

- Technology Review—another MIT offshoot. Offers articles and speculation on emerging, winning technologies. (www.techreview.com/)

develop your defensive strategy, assess your opponent's weaknesses

business development in a highly competitive and fast-paced environment is different from the business development of the old-style economy. Traditionally, businesses are slowly assembled, nurtured, and expanded. Unless you offer a fantastically cheaper solution, market share usually is captured only as you prove yourself to others in your market space. Rewards also come slowly as you become trusted and as you consistently provide competitive price, service, and selection to your customers.

In a new-style economy, first movers capture huge market share in a matter of weeks, and sometimes price, service, and selection are not even part of the mix. Inferior products sometimes win over better ones because they arrived first or were partnered with the right people.

Has the world changed so much? Actually, no. The traditional rules of business still apply as the balloon burst of the .com world proved. The so-called new economy is simply a land-rush economy of the type the world has endured many times in history. It seems like a radical change because we are more accustomed to the rules of a mature, established market. Internet spaces will become like this in time.

The previous chapter discusses the importance of boldness and staking your claim during a land rush. But during a shifting landscape, defensive posturing is equally important. You also must protect your assets. It's tough being the big dog on the block if you're not getting enough to eat.

If you boiled down a winning business strategy to just two lines, they would be

1. **Do what you can to make yourself invulnerable.**

2. **Wait for your opponent to be vulnerable, then attack.**

This seems fairly simple. But how do you achieve that perfect mix? There is no single formula, just as there's no single correct way to paint or play jazz. Business positioning is an art form. But there are definitely ideas and attitudes that indicate you're in good shape. You can be nearly invulnerable, or truly invulnerable.

• **You are *nearly* invulnerable if you have customer loyalty.** If your customers always look to you first to solve a problem or purchase a product, then you have a great defensive position. But maintaining this position is hard work. You must consistently please. Your products must remain top-notch, and your customer service must be excellent. You must always be a problem solver so that those with problems continue to come to you for the solution.

• **You are *nearly* invulnerable if you operate a reliable, easy-to-navigate Web site that helps people find the products they seek, and processes their transactions easily and securely.** Most people are lazy creatures of habit. They will return to the place where they've found success before. You can preserve a decent business simply by retaining repeat customers. Yes, there always lurks the threat that someone will come along and do things better. They may slowly siphon away your customers. And if other places offer significantly cheaper goods, even your lazy customers may exert the effort to find a new supplier. But if you can stay competitive, pricewise, you'll retain your nearly invulnerable status. Some businesses do this by forming buyers cooperatives that allow several businesses to buy inventory in bulk to achieve volume discounts like big national chains.

• **You are _nearly_ invulnerable if you offer the correct type of personalization for your customers, providing leads to the information and products they want without spamming them mercilessly with worthless pitches.** This level of personalization should not be limited to just your Web site. It should also extend to your sales force in the field. You can extend the relationship to track buying habits and inventory predictions via the customers' own data, learning all sorts of nuances about them until you become a conduit for their needs and the guardian angel of their business. That sort of working relationship is so rare, that customers will stay with you once they've found it.

But, like any other relationship, the fantasy is rosier than the reality. You will not always be the perfect partner. You will stumble at times. You will not always point your customers in the perfect direction because the way will not always be clear to you. They may be seduced by other promises. Thus, being _nearly_ invulnerable may not be enough. You want ironclad invulnerability. (Keep in mind that invulnerability doesn't last forever.)

• **You are truly invulnerable if you own a proprietary technology that everyone needs.** Examples of controlling what people need are owning the only bank, gas station, or airport in a small town, or owning a core architecture around which everyone else builds their products, such as Microsoft Windows. The best position is to own a technology that everyone else has to license. Check the driver software for the mouse attached to your computer. Chances are it comes from Logitech. If not, Logitech likely created and licensed at least part of that software. Talk about owning a cash cow. If you own such a key technology, you are invulnerable until someone makes a major, risky investment to build a competing service. Worse yet is when someone builds a nonproprietary technology that competes with yours, and offers it for free. (In the early 1990s, there were several attempts to sell graphical navigation for the Internet. Sprint was an early developer. But the first true Web browser, the freely available Mosaic, killed those other efforts.)

- **You are truly invulnerable if you have a product that makes you a recognized best of breed.** For example, EMC, the giant computer storage system manufacturer, has been on a steady growth curve for years. The need for computer storage continues to expand at many companies. Even though competitors offer cheaper, open-architecture, centralized storage systems, managers of high-end networks continue to flock to EMC because they offer a fantastic, highly reliable product. People buy EMC because they want the best.

Best of breed doesn't necessarily mean high-tech. Perhaps you are a fastener manufacturer who makes the strongest screws or bolts at a good price. Perhaps your best product isn't even the highest profit center of your business at this time. You might make more money from your molly bolts or your wing nuts. But if you have a best-of-breed product, people will find you, and you then have a powerful engine to serve as the core around which you can expand all parts of your business.

- **You are truly invulnerable if you are a market maker.** You then control a place in which everyone must come to you to do business, and you can extract fees for that service. Stockbrokers are often called market makers. But why stop there? Even bigger market makers hover above them. Can you imagine owning NASDAQ? Or the New York Stock Exchange? In the future, more and more products will look like commodities, and can be traded as such. We see this transition already for products like computer memory chips, which experience almost daily price fluctuations. If you can build the market where such new commodities are traded, you became a powerful market maker.

Who'd have thought something as arcane as antiques and collectibles could become commodities? But virtual marketplaces have been established, which pushed them from yard sales and dusty antique stores onto the radar screen of the general public. The largest such marketplace is eBay, where you can bid for anything from Tiffany lamps to 30-year-old *Mad* magazines. Print and online catalogs list prices for coveted items, and there is enough of each that buyers have a good idea of supply, demand, and price fluctuations as they make their bids.

Identify a commodity. Become a market maker for those who buy and sell the commodity, and find yourself in an invulnerable position.

• **If you are a media company, you are truly invulnerable when you own the content everyone else wants, especially if you distribute it at a reasonable price.** The Business Wire service created a powerful niche by collecting company press releases and feeding them to news organizations. They then extended their reach by offering the same feeds to online stock news and trading sites. (Look up any publicly traded company on Quicken.com, and you'll see a list of recent press releases from the company.)

As the Web grew, the Reuters news service made great inroads against the Associated Press by offering its news feeds to major Web portals at a very competitive price. Meanwhile, NewsEngin takes a much different approach, providing software that allows newspapers to build their own news databases from multiple sources. It includes tools to publish the news internally or to Web pages. Other businesses found success buying content feeds from multiple providers, segmenting them by subject, and then repackaging them as new feeds for specialty Web sites, or by creating popular chat areas or message boards that built a reliable following, then distributed access to those areas across other Web sites.

Information is a commodity, too, but the highest-quality and timeliest data carry a premium. Whoever controls the downstream flow controls the pricing of the most valuable data. Like anything else, news and information can be turned into a product. That's what your local newspaper is, and it's very difficult for anyone to displace a major metropolitan paper because of the huge investment required to build such an infrastructure.

• **You are truly invulnerable if you are a public company that does two things—consistently maintains a profit-to-earnings ratio (P/E) that is low for**

your industry, and consistently maintains a respectable growth rate. While these don't assure long-term invulnerability by themselves (because changes in technology and market conditions could hamper future growth), they do indicate that company managers are adept at long-term planning, cash-flow management, and predicting their return on investment. The only factor that will shake such a company is a change at the helm.

P/E is a simple (some may say overly simple) way to use the earnings of a company to assess the value of its stock. To figure P/E, divide the stock's price by its earnings per share for a 12-month period. For example, a stock selling for $50 that earned $5 a share for the year ($1.25 per quarter) has a P/E ratio of 10. Most Internet companies don't fall anywhere near this range. They are lucky if they're under 200. Arguably, a low P/E is more a requirement for older, established companies than for new companies. Internet stocks are highly vulnerable but highly rewarded as they grow. They are growth stocks. A low P/E company is usually considered an income stock because it's no longer rapidly expanding and sinking most of its profits back into the business. Instead, an income stock achieved its growth and dominance and rewards conservative investors with predictable dividends. Often, people prefer growth stocks as a long-term investment when they are younger because there's more upside potential. They prefer income stocks as they near retirement, because price stability protects their capital and the quarterly payments provide steady income. If a company eventually migrates from a growth stock to a low P/E income stock, it indicates the company's stability and maturity. A P/E below 25 is respectable in most industries. Some established industries are even lower. While that seems stable, these older companies sometimes have trouble attracting investors looking for huge upside potential.

In September 2000, Ford, GM, and DaimlerChrysler all had P/Es below 10, while high-flying .com companies like Yahoo and Lycos had P/Es well over 300. eBay's P/E topped 750. All three of these .com companies are relatively new compared to the auto companies. They are higher-risk/higher-reward growth stocks. None of these Internet stalwarts are likely to be displaced from their perches. But because their industry is still in its consolidation phase (and because new technologies plus product consolidations are complicating the industry consolidation), these companies remain more vulnerable than huge established manufacturers, which are harder to overtake. America Online, with its merger to Time-Warner, is an example of a growth company that's beginning to migrate to a traditional company. AOL's P/E dropped to under 120 by September 2000. Time-Warner income should drive that even lower.

But watching P/E alone isn't enough. A company might show great numbers several quarters in a row because it's selling off its key assets. Is this a company you'd want to own? Probably not, unless you think it's worth more broken up and sold than its share price indicates. In most cases, such a company is very vulnerable for the long term. Thus, you also want to look at a company's growth rate, even though this is harder to calculate than P/E. An easy way to judge growth is to look at investment sites. Look not only at the analyst ratings for a company, but also at the earnings-per-share predictions going forward for the next few quarters. Do these show a steady climb? Do they flatten out after a year? Do the analysts concur that growth is sustainable?

When investing, tradition says you should look for low P/E companies with predicted steady growth. There are even more complicated solutions for judging growth rates, but they would fill this book. A good place to start if you want to work out your own formula is to visit the Motley Fool Web site at www.fool.com. Look for the Fool School section on how to value stocks. Besides learning what to measure, you'll learn that a competitive, profitable company on a steady climb will always find buyers for its stock, which helps the stock hold its value, reducing short-term fluctuations and vulnerability.

These key positions limit a company's exposure and affect a good defensive posture. These, plus an eye on market and technology shifts, will keep a company strong and well positioned. But what if you don't fit any of the categories previously outlined? What other choices do you have for giving yourself at least the appearance of a strong defensive position?

Invincibility depends on you and your focus on yourself. Even without superior positioning, you can look like a formidable foe that is hard to displace. Do this by showing you can turn a profit, react quickly to challenges, and retain customers even as others try to lure them away. If you look like a business that will work long hours, lower your prices, and stop at nothing to protect yourself, predatory competitors may look elsewhere. It's like the small business owner who decides it might be too difficult to directly challenge the diner down the street and elects to open an ice cream shop instead.

Using Technology to Strengthen Your Defensive Position

You can also focus on the technology you'll need to protect your service. **As you move into e-commerce, make your systems as fault tolerant as possible to achieve near-perfect uptime.** A Forrester report estimated that downtime for e-commerce sites resulted in a loss of about $9,000 per hour in 1999. Major retail sites could lose well over $100,000 per hour.

Many companies sell supposedly fault tolerant or non-stop systems to reduce such downtime losses, but these can be haunted by lockups after simple system upgrades or plagued by RAM memory leaks that force the machines to be rebooted every week or so. Fault tolerant does not mean no downtime.

The way to build a bulletproof system is to take a cue from the way major Web portals built their sites. Most use Internet protocols and load-balancing features to shuffle traffic onto multiple front-end servers. These front ends, in turn, can pass queries to a central database or e-commerce system. Most likely, these services are also mirrored to multiple machines.

It can cost $7 million to build a system like this, and $2 million to

$3 million annually to maintain and upgrade it. That's on top of your application costs. Today, that kind of investment is only for the major players. But smaller companies are starting to take the plunge as a defense measure, realizing if they lose a customer just one time, that customer may never return.

Once you're confident about your systems, look for ways to expand your online marketing efforts. According to a Forrester report, most online marketing today goes into adding information and depth to corporate Web sites or extranets. It's not spent developing creative marketing approaches via third-party sites nor used to trade services for distribution across multiple outlets. Thirty-five percent of interviewees had not yet extended their online presence beyond a single site. Only 26 percent could cite a successful online campaign that drove new business.

Yet the infrastructure is in place for this. The simplest way is to swap advertising space with other sites. More complex methods include setting a cookie for every visitor sent to you by a certain site. You can offer those visitors a customized view of your data because they came from an approved site. You can also display the other company's logo in a cobranded environment, making the visitor think the place they came from has a very special relationship with you. (Had they arrived at your site via a different click stream, they might not see cobranding at all.)

People may pay to establish such special relationships with you, or you can pay for cobranding on other sites if it extends your reach and brand.

Finally, your best defense is to have a clear understanding of what is going on consistently in your organization. But the view of your inventory is only as good as the data and how often it is updated. You should push yourself to develop ever more dynamic systems that update your databases in real time. If you batch process all orders at night, you may not know you're sold out of an item until the next day, when you could have ordered it immediately. Better yet, your system could have ordered it for you.

There are many proprietary solutions for real-time data gathering, but the Internet in general seems to be settling on the Extensible Markup Language (XML) as a standard for universal data sharing.

XML is actually a trio of specifications. The basic XML 1.0 is a set of recommendations that explain the syntax of the metalanguage. The second part is a linking language that describes link relationships between documents. The third part is an extensible style language for using style sheets for various display devices.

This is a fancy way of saying that XML is a data format, not a document format. It allows certain parts of a document to be tagged, inserted, or extracted and controlled as needed. The two main uses for XML are locating specific types of data embedded in documents, and generating and updating documents from data that resides in databases.

Groups of developers can collaborate using their own customized tags. For example, your industry may decide that part numbers should be tagged as <partnumber>47861HB7</partnumber> or inventory might be tagged as <instock>27</instock>. The < > and the </> indicate the beginning and end of the tagged data. Different industries, such as auto manufacturers and insurers, have worked together to create their own tag sets. With such tagging, anything can become a data field, which significantly changes our traditional view of what a database is and how it's constructed.

But imagine the advantages of tagging data once and having it universally recognized across documents and databases. In the future, you might see a single entry shared across several government databases. An entry at the Social Security database automatically updates an IRS database and simultaneously updates a document at the Bureau of Labor Statistics.

At this time, the United Nations is working to produce a global XML framework for trade. It's working with OASIS, a Boston-based, international, nonprofit consortium dedicated to product-independent data and content interchange. Details can be found at www.oasis-open.org.

To track other XML efforts, the main activity page for the World Wide Web consortium's XML efforts can be found at www.w3.org/XML/Activity. Making a transition now to XML could be one of the best defensive moves you make for the long haul.

Waiting and Watching

Okay, so you've taken care of your own vulnerability. Now, what about the enemy's vulnerability? **Just as your level of vulnerability depends mostly on you, your opponent's vulnerability depends on the enemy.** It's usually not something you can directly influence. The most skilled businessmen can make themselves invincible but cannot cause their opponents to become more vulnerable, unless they can hire away all their best workers or steal their prized technology. Even then, there's the possibility of lawsuits. The lesson here is that you may know *how* to win, but you may not be *able* to win if you don't have the right opportunities to make your move.

Since we've focused so much on the importance of supply chains, Manugistics Group is a perfect example of the challenge of defensive posturing and waiting for the right time to break out. In the spring of 1998, the Rockville, Maryland, company was flying high. Its stock price shot up from around 40 to just over 80. It helped large corporations gather data from across their enterprises to create intelligent supply chain optimization solutions, and it was becoming a major player in a special niche for application software developers.

But it's very difficult to defend a niche in a market that's still evolving. By the end of 1998, Manugistics' stock price dropped back to under 20, where it remained for the next year while other players like i2, Optum, Oracle, Ariba, and Baan grabbed headlines, market share, and fantastic growth. Manugistics did not defend its position well, and it was apparently not astute at judging the vulnerabilities of its key competitors.

Or was it?

By mid-2000, Manugistics was on the comeback trail. Greg Owens, who took over as CEO in mid-1999, told reporters he inherited a company with good products and technical skills, but with limited marketing abilities. That's what he focused on first. Getting the word out. Defending the company. Explaining to customers what Manugistics does and how it could help large-scale manufacturers and service providers. This kind of marketing is extremely important for technical solutions providers because their products are not easy to understand.

Manugistics also successfully defended the core of its business. Its main customer base, through good times and bad, was and continues to be retail and transportation markets, while Manugistics' competitors focused more on high-tech manufacturers. Manugistics' killer defensive move came in the fall of 2000, when it merged with Talus Solutions, a yield-management software vendor focusing on pricing and revenue optimization. In plain language, Talus looks at clients' data flow, then develops pricing strategies to maximize revenue. Several airlines use Talus-developed systems to optimize capacity usage, which helps them eliminate unprofitable routes and increase profits from their other routes. By acquiring this system, Manugistics could apply the same technology to other transportation sectors, like trucking companies who need flexible pricing, a view of how price adjustments play out over long- and short-haul routes, and guidance to where they need additional routes. All such data can be shared between partners over limited extranets.

The move was a good one. Manugistics' stock price jumped 24 percent the day the deal was announced. Without directly challenging other supply chain stalwarts, Manugistics confirmed its long-awaited comeback, solidified its control over a key sector, and told the world of its intent to target the so-called midmarket of the B2B space—the small- and medium-sized businesses that have been overlooked by the fast-lane players.

A good defense is sometimes a game of patience. Manugistics preceded this big move by a year of small- and medium-sized deals, partnerships, and announcements. In an instance where you are extremely ready but unable to find a time when your opponent seems vulnerable, your progress has to be measured in small increments. In these times, keep yourself well defended and make tiny attacks when and where you can. Your opponent can't be everywhere, so patiently steal tiny bits of business where you can. Slowly, you will grow as you wait for the opportunity to make a big play.

> Sun Tzu says, "One defends when his strength is inadequate; he attacks when it is abundant. Those who are skilled in defense hide themselves as under the ninefold earth; those in attack flash forth as from above the ninefold heavens. Thus, they are capable both of protecting themselves and of gaining a complete victory."

The general advises be ready to fight, and be ready to avoid a fight. Your circumstances dictate which path is best. Be ready to dig in and protect your core business and skills. Be prepared to swoop down hard when you detect an advantage, whether it's to steal directly from your opponent or, as in Manugistics' case, to merge with a perfect partner and stake a claim on an underserved market niche. Having such patience and recognizing such opportunities is what makes a company truly great, especially in times of forced consolidation like we see today.

Achieve this by paying attention to market research that closely examines all areas where you do business, and all research that affects the things you buy. If you can't afford to purchase expensive research reports, remember there is a secondary market where you can pick up much of this information. The secondary market is news reports, trade journal interviews, and online message boards where information from such reports is extracted, analyzed, and discussed. Sometimes you can learn as much here as you can by reading the detailed reports.

Generally, it does not require great skill to read market conditions, view stock analyst papers, or scour public opinion surveys and then predict victory. Seeing what everyone else sees takes no particular talent in business. But finding a new target and hitting it does demand talent and hard work, especially while taking care of other routine business matters.

Likewise, you are no great business whiz if you triumph in battle when you are already the big dog in the neighborhood. Your momentum carries you, not necessarily your superior strategy. Such a win is no great test of your business vision or your company's virtue.

In fact, a company who always wins victory after victory without erring probably conquers smaller opponents who were halfway defeated already. These easy meat companies likely never worked to make themselves invincible. Or perhaps they were wreckable because they were old-school organizations who never adapted to the electronic economy or learned how to use it to defend their core business and customers while seeking new customers and markets.

The skillful CEO is one who finds herself in an underdog position and manages to make herself less vulnerable. A skillful corporation is one that cannot be defeated and which misses no opportunity to overcome a stronger enemy when vulnerable moments are sensed. Thus, a wise and ultimately victorious organization only seeks battle after observations and plans indicate that the time is right to move—because victory is possible.

The best opponent to target is one that fights in the hope of winning but without any detailed plan of action or understanding of how a market is changing. Such an opponent has no idea how customer needs can be met in a new environment. Think back to the early days of the Net. Companies that were slow to adopt e-mail lost business to those who could better communicate with new customers. Those who were slow to adopt online ordering also lost business to those who moved quickly. Organizations who lack this focus, but fight anyway, are destined to defeat.

If you make yourself invincible for your core competency, and if you adhere very strictly to the laws, regulations, and basic rules of business, it is in your power to build out from whatever key kernel of greatness you do possess.

In the early days of the Web, and even today, people sought the sweet spots that showed a broad user base seeking a specific type of information or product. If they could create an e-commerce niche around that, so much the better. But an e-comm niche has to extend beyond simple sales.

CNET's Comyns shares that viewpoint on creating commerce via a community niche. In Comyn's theory, the bottom of the e-commerce business consists of simple online transactions like books, music, or video. "They are low-ticket items," he said. "It doesn't take a ton of due diligence to buy them. You don't spend a lot of time doing research just to save a dollar."

That market plays nicely into a company like Amazon, who offers good prices and a great experience. Amazon is the only intermediary between you and the publisher. On the highest end are places like Car-Point or AutoWeb. Here people spend $20,000 or sometimes much more. "Are you going to do a lot of research before making that purchase? Absolutely," said Comyns. "Are you going to use your credit card to purchase that online? Absolutely not."

Between Amazon and CarPoint, CNET found a sweet spot of a $400 to $1,000 technology product. These are mostly peripherals and some full computers. People can employ due diligence and find sellers on CNET, though they don't really buy there. And advertisers are willing to pay one of the highest rates in the industry for a good click-through from the CNET site.

CNET leveraged this position when it bought the massive ZDnet site in summer 2000. It acquired even more content for its site in the form of article archives for the range of computer publications offered by ZDnet.

Competitive online publishers want to find similar sweet spots. They want to provide due diligence for people. They want to offer a

Consumer Reports–type resource that draws people and advises them. Visitors to such sites want to see user opinions and latest prices. They want to be comfortable using their credit cards through the site. Anyone who can provide all these elements has a shot at becoming a market maker in that industry.

> Sun Tzu says a victorious organization is like an ocean unleashed against a single drop of water. That drop is consumed and the flood continues on its path. Likewise, a defeated army is like one drop of water set up to hold back an ocean. It can't accomplish so huge a task.

A victorious company can likewise release its workers, capital, and technologies to push aside a minimal effort made by a challenger. If you unleash your best resources and follow a detailed plan, you will be a difficult organization to stop.

Set Priorities and Become Invincible

Do you remember the popular poster that was copied and recopied and hung in small businesses around the country? It was particularly prevalent at shipping and receiving desks where shifting workloads and late deliveries were the norm. The poster said something like, "When you're up to your ass in alligators, it's hard to remember that your original objective was to drain the swamp."

The message is clear. Sometimes you must resolve big problems before you can deal with little ones. Sometimes you must defend yourself first, and then worry about other work. Moving in Internet time, it's sometimes easy to forget this. Your competitive instinct tells you to concentrate on the next big thing, when what you need most is to get your own house in order first.

Finding the right mix of offense and defense is tough. Just don't forget to protect your key assets as you venture in search of new online business.

Tools

Following are simple steps you can take to ensure you are protected and plan your next move, even if you have to wait for the right time to execute that move.

- **Measurement—the size of the market space upon which you will compete.** How fast is that market growing? What are the market conditions? Who controls the space? Is it growing by dollars spent, number of people in the market, or both? Is the space new, or is it maturing? Will growth continue or will it level off or even shrink? (Use the research sources outlined at the end of Chapter 3 to gather this information.)

- **The estimation of quantities—what are the dollars spent here?** Who has resources ready to unleash to capture or defend this space? You should also measure the resources possessed by both you and your opponent and note how they are targeted. Perhaps you can't outspend the other guy in a head-to-head advertising campaign, so your money might be better spent picking up distribution through a third party, especially if that partner targets a growing segment your opponent doesn't reach.

- **Calculation—simple math.** After you know who has what, spend the time to run the numbers and figure some trends. How can your opponent target the market? What is their payoff? Is it worth it for them? Run the same numbers for yourself, and calculate your return on investment.

- **Comparisons.** Can you capture this space and achieve a higher ROI than your opponent? Can you sustain whatever market share you capture? Do you notice areas that your opponent is not targeting where both total customers and money spent per customer are on the rise?

- **Chances of victory.** This is an answer that comes from your calculations. Only you know what's acceptable for your own ROI, but if you can win market share and sustain service to those customers, then you can whittle away your opponent's advantages. Who is better suited to serve a specific niche, you or your opponent? Are there any advantages based on proximity, partnerships, or technology?

All Warfare Is Based on Deception

Time and time again, leaders win battles by deceiving their opponents. Sun Tzu's suggestions for deception are listed in the following, followed by modern examples.

- **"When capable of attacking, feign incapacity."**

The lesson is simple. When you are capable of challenging an opponent for market share—with a competing product, new technology, staffing addition, or marketing campaign—don't make it obvious you are equipped to make threatening moves. Don't make your opponent think defensive maneuvers are necessary. Don't look like a threat. Don't make it obvious that you have the workers, tools, and drive to execute a specific business plan. Your attack, when it's ready, will be more effective if it's unsuspected. Be aware, though, that there may be times you will need to let the competition know you are tough and capable. It might be an effective way for you to scare other competitors away. Or you might be able to force your competition to overcompensate for your strengths by spending too much on infrastructure and development, and thereby waste precious time and resources. Remember, the United States was able to drive the old Soviet Union to spend more and more money on its military—to the point of near bankruptcy—just by appearing stronger and acting more capable of attacking.

- **"When active in moving troops, feign inactivity."**

If you're going to make a move to capture a new market space, don't advertise your movements until you are in place and ready. Don't give the current owners of that market space the opportunity to know they're being challenged. Don't let others know you think a specific product, audience, or technology is worth a fight from a business standpoint. But how do you keep such movements quiet? Word can get out if you are looking for new hires. Real-estate agents know when you're looking for new office space (and boy, do they talk). Simply registering a domain name or buying new servers alerts someone, somewhere, that something is up.

The joke in Washington, DC, for years has been that you can tell something big is happening when you see an increase in the number of late-night pizzas delivered to the Pentagon or the White House.

To cover your tracks, you can have others do the leg work for you, giving them minimal details on what the effort is for. The person scouting for office space doesn't need to drop your name until the deal is signed. Equipment can be purchased in other names. Your help-wanted ads don't have to mention a company, though a name can be helpful for attracting the best employees. Be specifically vague when you advertise for new hires. Everyone knows the market potential for something like streaming media. Perhaps you're looking for Oracle database developers or people with experience in streaming media. Don't say, "We're looking for database developers to help us build a new online archive of classic movies that can be delivered via WebCasting." If your competition knows you are moving in on this market immediately rather than next month, they will react fast. Maybe faster than you can. Loose lips blow business leads.

Finally, be cagey when talking to potential partners or acquisition candidates. They will know you are interested, but they don't need to know where they fit in your overall business plan.

- **"When near the enemy, make it seem that you are far away; when far away, make it seem that you are near."**

This is a lesson from traditional warfare that doesn't, at first glance, translate to the Internet age. Space and time are compressed on the Net. A Web server in Europe answers a query about as fast as a server in Australia. Traditional distance doesn't matter. What does matter is how close you are, relationship-wise, to your enemy's customers. Remember, the territory you are conquering on the Internet isn't physical space. It's eyeballs, visitors, market share, trust, and commerce opportunities.

The train station analogy in business is a favorite. In the old economy, the coffee shop closest to the train station did more business than the one two blocks away. In the new economy, customers can reach your online shop about as quickly as any other shop. But location continues to matter in that the new location is distribution. Can customers find you via a search engine? If they started by looking for widget makers in California, would they still be willing to buy widgets from you in Timbuktu if they knew you offered a better price and free shipping? Can you get in front of them so they notice you? Partnering with the proper navigation hubs and content distribution partners is one way to do that.

There are other parallels between old and new. A close army can attack quickly. A distant army cannot. Thus, when close, you don't want your enemy to know you are close, so that you maintain an element of surprise. When you are far away, you don't want your enemy to know you are far away—they will feel complacent and seize control of an area you want to control. The parallel in .combat is this: While the Web is unlimited in size and time and while the space across this vast terrain is compressed, resources are not unlimited. You need to base your business in an area where you can capture the talented employees you need. You may need to host your machines at the same regional service provider your opponent uses because it offers the highest bandwidth in the region and the fastest response time.

Likewise, if you know you are out of the loop for a time, with no new products in the pipeline and no visionary employees building insanely great products, you can still look like a player who is breathing down your opponents' necks. Make appearances at trade shows, even if you don't have a booth. Walk the floor. Sit in on roundtable discussions. Be quoted in trade journals. Be quoted in the general media. Look like you're in the game even if you're on the sidelines for a time.

Getting others to link to you, host your content, or promote your brand, is key to getting noticed and capturing business. If people can see and find you in many ways, you have closed the distance between your customers and you. Use distribution, in the new economy sense (presence on multiple Web sites), to regulate distance and awareness.

Sun Tzu's lesson holds true. It's foolish to announce that you're going after a certain kind of business until you've already closed in on it.

Ask yourself if potential customers in your market know you. Do they know what you do? Do they need what you have and can you deliver it? You can work to make a name for your business and get customers to trust you before your opponent knows how close you are. Once you've grabbed a foothold, go ahead and issue that press release, and get back into the game.

- **"Hold out baits to lure the enemy."**

Just like you, your opponent is looking for an easy kill. You can make them think you're going after something lucrative when you are not. They may waste time developing applications to challenge you for that market space only to discover you were never really interested. This is a double whammy if you already knew through research that the space isn't lucrative.

In other instances, perhaps you can discuss partnerships and technology swaps with them, even though you don't intend to follow through. You can influence their distribution plan and affect their business. If you are competing with a company that's smaller than you, they probably would love a partnership with you. Large computer companies have been known to court multiple small companies, convincing each to work with them, influencing them to change their business models and processes or even their technology in order to achieve some possible deal with the larger partner. But then no deal is signed, or it's greatly reduced, and the smaller company is in trouble because it bet too much on an evolving possibility. If you are the smaller company, be wary of this approach. Pursue the partnership, but don't bet the life of your business on its outcome. Likewise, more than one content provider has failed to make money after signing a partnership agreement with a large Internet service provider. Promised traffic didn't materialize. Anticipated revenue share for advertising didn't happen. They took the bait and lost momentum from building a flawed partnership.

If you wish to avoid such baiting tactics, don't anticipate that a shared-risk/shared-reward scenario will boost your revenue. One good example is games developers who spend tens of thousands of dollars developing online games, hoping they'll make money if the games are hosted on paid portal sites. In such cases, they receive an ad revenue share, but there's no guarantee how much the ads will sell for, or even if the ad inventory for the games pages will sell out. Thus, if you're a games producer, it doesn't make sense to develop games strictly for a portal site. It makes more sense to develop your own separate business model and games pages that you control, and which you work to make profitable. Only then is distribution through a portal site as a second revenue stream a good choice. It's gravy on top of a hopefully profitable business that you've built and you control.

- **"Strike the enemy when he is in disorder. Prepare against the enemy when he is secure at all points."**

A chief cause of disorder is bad management. Immature technology, overly manual business processes, and an overall lack of product and market vision can exacerbate management problems.

Speed is paramount in an industry where first to market can add billions to your stock price. Without it, market share is lost. Disorder can trigger quick failure in rapidly evolving Internet markets. Disarray worsens as plans are thrown together haphazardly in order to get something out the door. This allows a better-organized company to move ahead. It gives competitive companies the thing they need most—an opportunity.

Other times of disorder are declining stock prices, management changes, relocation of offices, and long time lapses between product updates.

Today, database software maker Informix is making a comeback. Its profits are rising, and customers are buying its latest product offerings. But why must Informix make a comeback at all? What happened to this once-powerful company? The company stumbled badly amidst competition from its chief rival, Oracle. After a great run from the early to mid-1990s, Informix's sales slowed, and profits dipped in 1997. It didn't move as quickly as Oracle to build new programming tools and Internet interfaces for its products. Meanwhile, the Securities and Exchange Commission alleged that Informix executives had inflated the firm's financial performance from 1994 through mid-1997. These obstacles dragged down an otherwise powerful company with respected products. Oracle gained market share and momentum during this period of disarray.

The new Informix is very much betting its future on Internet applications. It has introduced an Internet-enabled database, called Foundation 2000, and a modular electronic commerce solution called iSell. But whether Informix can catch up to market leader Oracle remains to be seen.

The most likely cause of disorder for most businesses is changes to or rethinking of a product line or management structure. Other times of disorder come when a business is consolidating its operations, combining offices, losing people to attrition, and executing new operations or marketing plans that take time to gain traction. Take advantage of these if you can.

If the opponent is strong, ordered, and easily dominating the market space you want to invade, prepare not only your plan of action, but for the best time to execute it. Decide how you will move when you sense disarray and hesitation.

- **"Avoid the enemy for the time being when he is stronger."**

In the business realm, this doesn't mean you should not stop by their booths and trade shows to get a close look at their products or discuss joint development efforts or partnerships. It means you should avoid directly challenging the opponent in an area where you know they are stronger. Wait and try to sense when a better time might be. If you don't see a good time to directly challenge, it may mean that, in the meantime, you should adjust your business plan and focus on a different niche.

AOL is the dominant Internet service provider and content distribution channel, and it offers services for a competitive price. Starting your own such service with the intention of displacing AOL would be ill-advised, especially if you don't offer something radically unique to draw satisfied customers away from AOL. A wise service provider will avoid a head-to-head confrontation with AOL. There are other niches to fill. Some of them might challenge a niche that AOL underserves and build a business by offering free Internet access. Some might find a way to partner with the giant, for mutually beneficial results, such as news services that feed content to AOL subscribers. And some might even let themselves merge with the giant for the right price, like Time-Warner did.

Anyone who's been involved in guerrilla warfare, or even guerrilla marketing, can tell you that you don't defeat a stronger opponent by attacking head-on. You stay away. You work the political angles and plan on your own. You challenge the stronger force only when you have to, and you hit and run against its weak, not its strong, points.

- **"If your opponent is of bad temper, try to irritate him or her."**

You can cause an enemy to waste time and resources answering challenges that anger him. If you perceive that your opponent has a big ego that hates bruising, and who will fight back, use that to your advantage to distract her from her main mission of running a profitable company.

Sun Microsystems' CEO Scott McNealy is a master at this game. He's been known to refer to archrival Hewlett-Packard as "a great printer company," purposely belittling HP's powerful Unix server and workstation products. He was also a constant thorn in the side of Microsoft as it fought the Justice Department for the right to remain whole. McNealy was even involved in a feud with Intel over a joint project to get Sun's Solaris operating system onto servers running Intel's newest processors. In that case, it was Intel that went on the offensive, saying Sun didn't pull its weight in the arrangement and threatening to drastically reduce its development resources. Jabs and a little focused anger irritated both companies and made them change direction and work toward a compromise.

You also can irritate a business by talking to their customers or hinting at problems. You can needle the opponent through advertising and trade magazine interviews. You need not refer to brand as long as you don't lie. Call a spade a spade. Get in their face. If your opponent is flustered, she may make mistakes, or at least she will be delayed as she deals with ego problems instead of business problems.

- **"If he is arrogant, try to encourage that egotism."**

A self-important CEO can sometimes become complacent. Encourage his vanity, and spend your time working while he primps. An arrogant CEO or company may doggedly go after only first-tier partners while those potential partners are more interested in alternative business arrangements with other companies. While it's important to be a market leader, plenty of good businesses work mainly with the second-tier businesses of their market space, and these companies can be very reliable and profitable. An arrogant opponent will not recognize when it's time to settle for second in one facet of the business in order to concentrate on becoming a first-tier player in another area. An arrogant opponent may throw good money after bad because her ego won't let her admit she made a bad business decision.

A good example of ego hurting business decisions is Seymour Cray, inventor of some of the fastest supercomputers ever built. It's probably not fair to label the late Cray as arrogant. He basically was a nice guy with a great passion for his work. But he always seemed happier in a lab than in a business suit, and it was his passion for developing cutting-edge technology at all costs that ultimately caused his problems. Cray built supercomputers during a period when the U.S. government and some industrial customers were willing to shell out $30 million for a high-end computer. But by the early 1990s, other companies were using cheaper, standardized processors to build massively parallel computers with nearly the same processing power as Cray's high-end machines—at about 25 percent of the cost. Yes, his big computers were still the fastest on the planet, but few customers were willing to pay significantly more for machines that were just a bit more powerful. It became obvious that Cray needed to produce cheaper hardware.

But he didn't change his focus. In order to achieve tremendous speeds, Cray continued to make big, fast processors that needed a flow of liquid nitrogen just to keep them cool. The cost of building and maintaining the machines was exorbitant. He knew he could build the fastest machines on earth. His ego wouldn't accept a compromise to build a cheaper machine. He had not changed his philosophy much since a 1974 speech in which he said, "In all of the machines that I've designed, cost has been very much a secondary consideration. Figure out how to build it as fast as possible, completely disregarding the cost of construction."

Cray Research eventually spun off a separate company for Seymour Cray in 1989, simply called Cray Computer. There, he could continue his cutting-edge development work, while Cray Research under new leadership started developing more cost-effective machines.

At the time of his October 1996 death in a car accident, Cray was working on a processor that reportedly ran at 1 gigahertz in a lab setting. At that time, the average PC ran at under 200 megahertz, and other supercomputers were lucky to hit 400 megahertz. Only at the end of 2000 did we see affordable processors that reached the speed of his 1996 project.

Cray's final project, the powerful but still too expensive Cray III, never made it to market. Only one Cray III computer ever saw long-term use, on loan to the federal government for weather prediction. Users said they were very satisfied with it, but Cray Computer as a viable business was finished.

Cray Research did live on. It was bought by Silicon Graphics and merged into its line of high-end computers. In March 2000, SGI spun the division off, and it merged with Tera Computing to form a new company called Cray, Inc.

Seymour Cray was right. He was very capable of finding innovations in order to remain the fastest of the fast. But at what cost? Perhaps he deserved a big ego because of his remarkable accomplishments. Computing would not be what it is today without people like him pushing the speed envelope to its extreme. But that doesn't always work hand-in-hand with good business sense.

In spite of his genius, Cray's ego and defiance of basic business rules ultimately doomed his chances. It's unfortunate he didn't live long enough to prove his doubters wrong by staying ahead of the pack.

Today, as in Sun Tzu's time, an opponent with a big ego may turn out to be an opponent with a big weakness.

- **"If they are united, try to sow dissension among them."**

You can make your opponent's employees work far into the night if they think that's what it takes to keep up with you. You can hire away their best workers by offering better pay and stock packages. If their stock price is stagnant, help the opponent's workers and others believe the company is also stagnant. If their stock price is climbing, make them believe all profits are going to a few managers instead of being shared by the workers.

Pay, work hours, whether the company is a true player, the wisdom of the CEO, the company's media portrayal, the relative coolness of their products or the technology used—these are all things that draw workers together or tear them apart. They are all talking points you can use to sow dissension in their ranks.

Surprisingly, news stories that quote tech-industry human resource executives have mentioned that one common reason for leaving a company is to join a player making a major contribution to a specific field. If you can't promise your employees a certain level of coolness or keep them in the industry spotlight, you better compensate them in other ways, such as bonuses and stock plans.

- **"If the enemy troops are well prepared after reorganization, try to wear them down."**

If you can't wait for disarray, sometimes you must cause it. You may have to make your opponent respond to you. Do this by planting rumors.

Do this with hit-and-run tactics that challenge their shifting marketing plan or their advertising focus. Openly challenge their technical knowledge or their ability to compete in the new economy. Make them respond. Make sure you have your facts straight and your own response prepared. Wear them down.

You can also make them think you are working on many different projects. They may think they need to work on the same things you are to protect their market share. Highlight any problem you see with their products or organization and make sure others know about it. Point out waste and overspending. You can busy them with trifles and make them doubt the wisdom of their reorganization.

- **"Attack the enemy where he is unprepared, and appear where you are not expected."**

This is no different in today's Internet culture than it was hundreds of years ago. The element of surprise always works in your favor. Add to this the new markets that are constantly evolving. Who would have guessed there was such a market for online auctions? eBay did, beating out a number of large competitors who were better prepared to build such an auction system—had they known what such a site would eventually be worth.

Ameritrade and E-Trade moved fast when older, larger brokerages like Merrill Lynch did not move quickly to a leaner and cheaper online business. Then, in their first years, these upstarts channeled a good portion of their revenue back into customer acquisition strategies to build market share.

There are hundreds of places where you can grab market share from a competitor and establish a new market where there was none before. Like the Boy Scouts, be prepared. It's your greatest advantage.

These rules of deception, combined with observations of the five fundamental factors and a good battle plan, are keys to victory for an Internet strategist. It is not possible to formulate all these factors in detail beforehand. In fact, being able to notice, think, and respond quickly is vital to success, which makes it difficult to set any of these items into a must-do list of ironclad rules.

And that will be your greatest challenge. Some of the conventions require you to think well ahead and have a detailed road map, while others basically require that you be ready to observe and make quick changes to your strategy.

Soldiers start with a battle plan. Not having a plan is suicide. But they also have to think fast and react fast once they are in the fog of war, and that may mean adjusting the plan.

Businesspeople must start with a detailed business plan, but they should enter the market with their eyes open and their sleeves rolled up. Situations change, and they change fast. The more detailed and situational your Internet business plan, the more likely you will know exactly why and how to deviate from that plan when the time comes. The decision will be easier.

Learning Your Strengths, Learning Their Weaknesses

If access drives the Internet, finding ways to provide access is what drives those who build Internet businesses.

Because building these businesses is a high stakes and very competitive game, it's extremely important to know as much as possible about your competition. Start by knowing what part of the access business they are in. What do they provide, and to whom? Is it access to products, services, people, or raw data? What value do they add to the access process? How do they extract a profit, and how much do they take? Can their prices be undercut by eliminating inefficiencies that you notice in their process? Only by knowing such things can you decide to avoid your competition, do an end run around them, force them into a partnership, buy them, or battle head-to-head with them, undercutting their service and stealing their business.

157

Likewise, if this business really is about software, as well as access, then software and other key technologies remain *the* crucial stronghold for any competitive company. Technological superiority is a strength with which it is difficult to compete. It's like a nation with nuclear weapons fighting a nation without that technology. If push ever comes to shove, there is no contest.

Technology is so important it's the first thing some venture capitalists look for when seeking new companies. A great business plan and golden management take second place.

Internet powerhouse CMGI of Andover, Massachusetts, has a mixed record in finding and funding fledgling companies and ideas, building some of them into Internet powerhouses, while others flounder and are eventually nixed. The CMGI @Ventures arm is a well-known incubator for new Net ideas. It's as famous in the New England area as Sand Hill Road is in Silicon Valley. Yet David Wetherell, CEO of CMGI, claims he's not a venture capitalist and CMGI isn't really an Internet incubator. After all, it has several operating companies under its umbrella. Still, few people have as much experience as Wetherell when it comes to identifying promising ideas and building them into Internet businesses.

So what does Wetherell look for in a potential Net business? "We get over 3,000 business plans per month," he told a gathering of Internet techies and executives in the fall of 2000. "We look for technology first. You'd better be a first mover solving a really hard problem. That's the single most important thing we look for. Also, if there is a barrier to entry for others, it creates an opportunity to get big fast. So, most often, we look for great technology first and great management second. After these, we look for something that's complementary to what we're already doing so we can help leverage it and ramp it up."

"Yet, you can't just sell technology for technology's sake," says Barry Schuler, president, Interactive Services Group, at America Online. "The technology has to do something that's needed and must be easy for consumers to use. Yes, it is a new economy. The Internet can do wonderful things. But we need to use those wonderful things to create value for businesses and people's lives."

So what business are you in? Software? Services? Do you possess, or can you develop, a key technology? Do you want to? Or are you more comfortable handling the integration of someone else's technology?

> **One key thing any leader can do to participate in this historic online expansion is appraise himself and his organization as mentioned in Chapter 1, to discover the strengths of his company. He must adjust accordingly. Once the strengths are known, they must be properly managed, especially as the company grows.**

One thing Sun Tzu stresses over and over again is that control of a large force follows the same principle as the control of a few men: It is merely a matter of dividing up their numbers, appointing leaders for the smaller groups, and then commanding a small group of leaders. But in a corporate setting, management can be more complex than that. For example, let's say you are a company that developed a software solution for delivering Web applications via cell phones. This is a relatively young marketplace, and your company isn't well known, but you're large enough to employ several regional sales teams, and three or four product development teams. A wise corporate leader knows that each team has different strengths, even if they share the same basic structure. Likewise, the people within the teams may also have unique strengths, leading to different configurations from within each team. On one team, a product manager may have great technical skills and do a great job doubling as an operations manager, supervising product development and production. On other teams, the PMs may have stronger marketing skills and feel more comfortable on the road, flacking the product to new markets and coordinating the sales teams and their plan of attack. Still other product managers may turn out to really be program managers. They are good at ramping up new products, but when the time comes to manage those products, they'd rather turn that task over to someone else and go back to square one, picking up a new concept and a new development challenge.

In such cases, the person who builds the teams must realize that adjustments are needed, and then add people to the teams who complement the ensemble and bring skills that the others lack. Too rigid a mentality in defining job titles means shoehorning talented people into positions where their best skills are not exploited. For example, some people are just better at solving problems and building things than they are at maintaining a finished product. If you have tunnel vision on what a product manager, marketing manager, programmer, or even an administrative assistant is or does, then you shut off opportunities to build a dynamic team that self-adjusts to dynamic markets. Obviously, you must staff employees who work well in a set structure in order to accomplish your business plan. But you might be surprised at how much you actually accomplish when you let your best people flex their talents.

A company has different strengths depending on how its teams are built and arranged. Ask yourself, have you arranged teams to properly leverage your best people? What do your teams do best? What can they accomplish?

One of Bill Gates's first products, pre-Microsoft, was a traffic counting system. But he found he had a talent for negotiating deals to develop technologies for the fledgling industry of personal computers. He essentially migrated from programming to business development. Sometimes knowing your personal strengths and the strengths of your employees gives you the confidence to set off in new, profitable directions. This is a very desirable trait in the fluid online world.

As companies grow, communications between employees, and between the company and its business partners, becomes more important. General Sun Tzu says fighting with a large army under your command is no different from fighting with a small one—it is merely a question of instituting signs and signals. This also applies to businesses. Each team must know its purpose. Each team must know its strengths.

Rather than stifling praise for fear of giving employees large egos, feed them the praise and support they need to continue developing their strengths. When a team knows it is strong and capable, it senses victory in its future and becomes a stronger force.

This is where flexibility in team building pays off. Each team knows exactly where it fits in an organization and what its duties are, so that efforts can become concentrated and focused. However, strong teams will sometimes extend into your other teams' turf in their efforts to prosper. This is not necessarily bad. It produces new ideas and new synergies. For example, product teams sometimes want to wear a business development hat because they may be the first to identify new opportunities for their product. Marketing people know what the market is looking for, and may try to influence product development, engineering, or sales. Someone in the trenches each day may be the first to spot a competitor that should be acquired. They may be the first to realize that sales are slipping and new sales channels must be opened. Letting people stray a bit outside their normal workflow can be beneficial, as long as they don't muck up an otherwise working process.

Some pure online companies, by the late 1990s, found they made no money in the page view game. They were expert at developing content, but not at managing services and selling ads. Often it was the people in the trenches, not the CEO, who first noticed this shift and nudged the companies in a different direction. Perhaps owning page views was less important than distributing content to others and getting paid for it. Who notices such things first? Who decides to make the change? Who actually changes the product to transition to a new niche?

Such decisions can create tension between teams. Should business development be its own separate section of the company? Or should each team in your organization include a business development person who works closely with product managers and key developers to identify promising opportunities and go after them? Neither is necessarily the correct approach. The company leader needs to take a good look at the structure of her teams and decide who has stronger talents for the necessary tasks, and allow some employees to step out of their defined box and into new territory.

To take advantage of a specific talent, certain bleedover into other teams' turf is inevitable, as is the friction it will cause. For example, the lowly Web artist on your catalog-building team, who happens to be from Pittsburgh, might become a key point person for your mergers and acquisitions team that's looking to acquire a company to serve that market, because they need to know demographic information and local nuances. Should the artist not be part of the team just because she's an artist?

Likewise, should a business development person not be allowed to change the look and feel of a product if he knows it could result in a new business deal worth millions? If you know the strengths of your teams and your team members, you will have an easier time making such decisions, and letting your best people and ideas rise to the top.

Know What They Don't Know

Just as one needs to build teams and leverage strengths, one needs to know the weaknesses of a competitor and exploit them. What areas are they underserving, and why? Is their failure a management issue, or a technical one? If you challenge them, how soon could they respond, and how easy will it be for them to fix their issues? Do you want to risk a major market push targeting a weakness that can be fixed quickly? A major technical issue can take a year to fix, but minor technical short-comings can be fixed in less than two months. Management shake-ups can quickly breathe new life into underserved markets. How much would you bet that the problems you see will or won't be fixed? There are other considerations. If your competitor is tapped financially, it may be difficult for them to hire the employees they need to fix their weaknesses. It could be that they are already on a slippery slope, and you can exploit their weaknesses unchallenged.

Knowing *all* of your competitor's weaknesses, be they financial, staffing, marketing knowledge, or technical prowess, can help you piece together the right decision about what to exploit and how much you will risk in the process.

Knowing strengths and weaknesses includes knowing what company you are in. "We know we are a software company," says Eric Levin, VP of marketing for Frictionless Commerce. "That's what we do. We give the software and tools to people who want to build the e-marketplaces. We don't build them ourselves. People with industry expertise usually build them, like a guy who has been in the tire business his whole life who wants to start E-tires Online. He knows the buyers and sellers. He doesn't want to develop the software to build the site."

That means both companies realize their strengths. The guy in the tire business knows tires and doesn't want to become a technical expert. He'd rather invest a few hundred thousand dollars for the foundation of an online marketplace that he can help populate with offerings and communities. Frictionless Commerce knows it would never have the expertise or industry contacts to build something like a tire marketplace. Its strength is building powerful marketplace-building tools, from importing real-time data feeds to online comparison shopping. (The company helped build the sprawling Lycos Shop area within Terra Lycos.)

Perhaps your opponent's weakness is simply that he does not know this. Perhaps, because of ego or ignorance, he is tackling too much by trying to build the software that will drive his e-marketplace, trying to reinvent what has already been invented. Your best defense may be to simply let him continue down that path.

In his book *Burn Rate: How I Survived the Gold Rush Years on the Internet*, Michael Wolff outlined the successes and failures of his online endeavors, including near-panicked cash shuffling and late nights trying to keep his start-up company going. It served as a warning and a wake-up call to other would-be Net entrepreneurs that building an online business isn't as simple as developing a decent idea and then taking a company public as soon as possible.

One of Wolff's opinions is that there are few successful business models based solely on the Web. Few people have been able to make it pay in a sustainable way. Yet investors continue to up the ante for Web investments, trying to corner the market on something they know will eventually be profitable. But for whom?

In general, burn rate is the rate at which a start-up company runs through its capital while ramping up operations and building a name for itself as it tries to reach profitability. Many Internet companies in the late 1990s were famous for spending valuable capital on high-profile marketing efforts instead of product development, increasing their burn rate by buying Super Bowl ads or throwing lavish parties in hopes of gaining name recognition.

Stereotypically, this type of spending is the mark of a company more interested in making a quick name, and then a quick killing, rather than a company investing in valuable technology and long-term growth.

For any company, the issue is whether revenue will grow to a sustainable level to fund operations and future growth before the initial invested revenue is burned through. If the burn rate exceeds projections, or if revenue doesn't meet expectations, the burn rate must be reduced by cutting staff, marketing efforts, or executive perks. Once the initial investment capital is burned out though, the company doesn't necessarily fold. Hopefully there was enough investment in technology or in gaining market share and perceived value, that the company can procure additional capital through new equity investors, a public stock offering, or by selling itself to another company at a price that will pay off the original investment, with change.

The best thing a struggling company needs to know is how to spend. Know how to leverage your strengths rather than succumb to the lure of creating an industry buzz for its own sake. "Many .com companies took big chunks of their initial funding and immediately bought TV ads," said AOL's Schuler. "I looked at those ads and I couldn't understand what any of them were about. They were unintelligible as to what they were selling. I asked a friend who worked at one of the companies, and he said, 'Yeah, but the ad is cool, don't you think? And we won awards for it!' I asked, 'But did you sell anything?' He answered, 'Well, we're not sure we bought the right time,' and other excuses. People need to realize that marketing fundamentals haven't changed. You have to communicate to people what benefit they will get out of something."

That's a lesson for all start-up companies. **Cool commercials don't necessarily bring new customers.** If you're advertising mostly for name recognition, studies show that repetition helps people remember a name more than making one big Super Bowl–size buy. Smaller buys using less-expensive ads over a longer period of time may be a better way to embed your name in people's minds. So do ads that help people understand what you do, and what that means for them. Whether you're a start-up company, an older company that's competing with young upstarts, or an investor watching these games as they play out, it's important to note which companies understand these points, and which have the weakness for burning through cash with little to show.

Once You Note the Weaknesses, Take Advantage

When you do see a weakness, decide how you can exploit it. Attack the weak points to assure yourself victory.

Sun Tzu says there are two types of attack. Direct and indirect. One is a head-on challenge. The other is affecting the behavior of your opponent. Both are effective. Both are necessary because you need to vary tactics and work like a wave, cresting and pulling back, always wearing away without wearing yourself down. It is sometimes the indirect methods that assure victory. You force your opponents to make decisions that will ultimately lead your opponent away from you, reducing your conflict.

Direct, then indirect, then direct again. Variation. Sun Tzu compares these changes to the sun and the moon, heaven and earth, the changing seasons, musical notes, even a rolling grindstone. His point is that variation is necessary, and can be used to your advantage when you have patience and endurance to carry them out. It is especially wise to seize an advantage during any lull.

There are also times when it might be best to remain neutral. If your market space is changing, if you see no logical direction, and if you are not a gambler, it may be time to hold off and not execute any plans. Portfolio managers for large investment firms know this. When a market is volatile, they make money two ways. They go long on stocks that are growing, and short sell the stocks that have run up too much and are due for a fall. But when the direction of the market isn't clear and a trader doesn't know where action is headed, they slowly increase their cash position. They sell stocks at high points and keep their money out of the game for a while. If they see only high-risk/low-reward plays, they go to cash instead. Most mutual fund managers keep about 4 percent cash at all times. In times of uncertainty, some may keep 10 percent cash, or even higher.

Yet neutrality is surprisingly difficult. People like to play the game. Market trends force you to make decisions. While laziness often means that you continue old habits, neutrality toward a technology or new business or market development does not signify laziness. It means you've taken the time to study both sides and decided there is not yet enough evidence to make an educated choice.

The Challenge of Staying the Course

Where you will face problems, as you vary between direct and indirect attacks, is when you become unfocused or, worse, reckless. This can lead to destruction because your opponent may be waiting for the right time to seize the advantage from you. A similar problem is lack of nerve, or what people used to call cowardice. Competing online is a tough game to play, with a lot of money at stake. One must have nerves of steel to face down the challengers. One must be able to sleep at night, even as hundreds of worries trickle through your thoughts. If you lose your nerve, or if you stand like a deer in the headlights, refusing to make a decision when one is indeed needed, your cause is lost and your market share will be captured.

Most often, though, lack of confidence is due to lack of research and planning. Make time for this. Be confident in your plan so that you can be bold in your execution, and stay away from emotional decisions that stray from a well-constructed plan.

You will encounter adversity as you execute your plan. This includes staff losses, financial losses, and technical setbacks. These will only become weaknesses if you have not prepared for them. (Remember earlier when we said failure should be part of your plan?) View adversity as part of doing business. Your setbacks are not a weakness others should be able to exploit. But you may be able to exploit such weaknesses in others, especially if they have not properly prepared for them.

If your setbacks do not greatly affect your burn rate because you are still following a predictable path, you will remain strong. If your opponent's burn rate seems to increase whenever they face setbacks, you may be able to seize an advantage by convincing their investors to invest in you instead, and by taking specific chunks of business they can't properly serve.

going into battle

time your strike: be the first to move

Sun Tzu says, "Generally, he who occupies the field of battle first and awaits his enemy is at ease, while he who comes later to the scene and rushes into the fight is weary."

In business, that's called the first mover into a new business niche. Yet here's a disturbing image for anyone who thinks being first mover is all it takes to succeed. Think of a drum major. Let's say you are the best drum major in the parade business, with a high step, a cool uniform, and a shiny baton that looks great when held high in the air. But unless there's a parade behind you, few people will stop and watch your act. In fact, you'll probably look rather foolish. That's why being first mover in business is such a tough call. You can't be a leader if nobody wants to follow.

Even if you see great potential for a lucrative business niche, moving into that niche and building a business there can be tough. What if no one else sees the potential? What if people do see potential, but also see other niches that look equally lucrative? The safer play is usually to wait and see if the new market niche starts growing and proving its viability. But by then, a dozen other first-mover wannabes will likely arrive before you.

Thus, the secret to being a first mover *seems* to be this: First movers are gamblers. If they bet early and bet right, they arrive to set up shop before everyone else. Good timing and a gambler's heart are often what it takes to get there first.

Take such a gamble, and you might be like the group who built Web servers before anyone knew Web servers would change the world. One of the first widely used Web servers was made by the National Center for Supercomputing Applications (NCSA) at the University of Illinois. But this early server needed several enhancements and patches. The Apache Web server effort grew from the early NCSA efforts. (The name evolved because it was, literally, a "patchy" server.) Today, enhanced Apache Web servers run on about half the installed Web servers in the world. That's a huge user base from something that started as a niche service. In this case, Apache is coordinated by the not-for-profit Apache Software Foundation at www.apache.org/. But the first-mover lesson should be clear to commercial enterprises and nonprofits alike. There was a need, a product was created to meet that need, and a huge user community formed around the product.

People who identify and take a risk to serve any new, evolving market become the first to occupy that market niche or field of battle. They can dig in, find the best partners for the new conquest, and earn an important home field advantage.

On the Internet, such markets evolve quickly. Their genesis can be hidden in places as obscure as message boards, search logs, or click-through numbers. These records can show what people need and hint at new products or services. Read the signs, move fast, and you might catch them, or even lead them.

Because it's risky to be a first mover, it's advisable to serve a new market with minimal initial investment. Luckily, serving these markets in their early hours is not difficult. Sometimes it can consist of little more than hosting directories or advertisements for that new community. The community either evolves or dissipates as the need increases or wanes. Business opportunities lurk in communities that evolve from nonprofit efforts, because at some point the community grows too large to be sustained by volunteer efforts. That's how so many other Web servers, besides the Apache server, grew out of those early NCSA efforts. They took a good product and improved it. This process is also how several Linux providers took root.

Linux remains freely available on the Internet. (Visit www.linux .org/ for a list of download sites.) But how can you make money from a free product? Enterprises like Red Hat, Corel Linux, and others built businesses not around selling Linux per se, but around packaging Linux for easy installation and configuration. They also offer service and support. PC manufacturers offer some models with Linux pre-installed, and they work with these Linux specialists to offer documentation and service contracts.

Earlier, we said first-mover status seems to belong to gamblers. But successful professional gamblers don't really gamble. They play the odds. You greatly improve your odds when you observe user communities building themselves via nonprofit efforts. Transferring any community from a nonprofit to a commercial service can be a challenge, because many members may be committed to the nonprofit roots. (That was certainly the case with many academics who blasted the eventual commercialization of the Internet.) But stalwart, never-go-commercial types are probably not the customers you're hoping to capture. When you can enhance an existing free service, new customers will come to you for the convenience you provide. The stalwarts in the community can continue to do . . . whatever it is they do.

Where do you find such communities heading toward commercialization? Look at government technologies that are being commercialized. Look at nonprofit associations that helped establish standards and processes. And look at mailing lists for evolving technologies to see who the key players are.

Here are some examples.

• NASA maintains a very useful site called the Center for Technology Commercialization at www.ctc.org/. They even offer assistance with corporate start-ups centered on a government-developed product.

• The National Technology Transfer Center is a government-sponsored project located at the Wheeling Jesuit University in West Virginia. With the slogan, "Today's Technologies—Tomorrow's Products," the center focuses on the commercialization of products, ideas, and technologies that grow out of government-funded research. Learn more at www.nttc.edu/.

• The Massachusetts Institute of Technology is a hotbed of research for new media applications. Start with the MIT Media Lab at www.media.mit.edu/. If you believe the future belongs to those who wear head goggles and data gloves, be sure to also visit the wearable computer's section at www.media.mit.edu/wearables/. Look also for MIT's *Technology Review* magazine. It's a fun read and a great place to discover who is building robots or tweaking molecules.

• MIT is also the home of the World Wide Web Consortium, headed by Web inventor Tim Berners-Lee. The W3C is a hotbed for new research and user communities that heavily influence the future of the Web. Details are available at www.w3.org/. You could become a first mover into a new Web technology just by monitoring new standards under consideration by W3C.

• The Small Business Administration is really focused more on helping small businesses than on identifying niche product development. But its outreach initiatives include a venture capital arm that targets low-to-moderate income areas. Combine this with SBA's tech development databases and you could have the genesis of a government-backed effort to leverage tech ideas for niche products.

• The Institute for Operations Research and the Management Sciences (INFORMS) maintains a Web site that allows operations management professionals to network and share new ideas. Visit www .informs.org/. The site's searchable database of working papers and presentations is a great place to uncover budding communities and technology solutions that can inspire opportunities.

• It you want to focus on identifying international high-tech opportunities, the U.S. Commerce Department operates the U.S. Commercial Service, which helps businesses leverage product concepts into worldwide user communities. Learn more at www1.usatrade.gov/.

• The nonprofit public policy organization known as RAND sponsors several science and technology research programs with ties to the Internet community. It's a great place to monitor research that identifies specific business needs. Visit www.rand.org/. Look for the Analysis for Business section.

• Internet.com is not only the neatest address on the Internet, it's a great research facility. It has news, reference resources, lists of deals, technology developments, and more. It's a place to take the pulse of businesses that rely on the Net and technologies that influence those businesses.

• Those expensive industry reports compiled by the Gartner Group, Forrester, and others sometimes contain gems of business data that can help you identify logical new opportunities. Read them if you can afford them. Get business partners to pass them on to you. But, by nature, these reports rely on past-performance data, and they extrapolate trends based on market surveys. That's good science, but it doesn't always help you notice any new whirlpools and eddies in the e-commerce river. Only direct participation in the process gives you that.

Here's a currently evolving example of how a technology change can build a community, and a community can become a marketplace. The Federal Communications Commission, as part of its E911 program, has dictated that cell phone companies must offer technology to locate callers to within about 100 meters by October 2001 (at least those callers who choose to participate in the program). That means cell phones capable of picking up signals from the U.S. Defense Department's Global Positioning System (GPS) are the newest big thing for cell phone product lines. It also means a user community has a new need—cell phone companies worked hard to merge GPS systems and phones, and continue refinement of those products, but that's only the tip of the new market.

Advertising for such systems is close behind. At no cost to you, your GPS-enabled cell phone can now beep to notify you the restaurant you're driving past gives 15 percent off to cell phone users. If you lack pocket change to buy from a soft drink machine, isn't it nice to know there's a phone-enabled Coke machine a block away that will let you dial it and charge a drink to your debit card? Conventions like Internet World are now filled with vendors pitching wireless solutions based on user proximity.

Communities already are forming around the ideas. One example is the Open Development Advisory Council (ODAC), set up to examine economic models for open-source software programs for computers, handheld and cell phone marketplaces. Learn more at www.odac.org/.

There are dozens of activities like the GPS ruling or the forming of ODAC that spur temporary communities. These groups bring all participants together as needs grow and solutions gel. Monitoring them can help you identify evolving needs, while reducing a good deal of the risk associated with first-mover status. You don't really move first. You simply move along with and just slightly ahead of the crowd to offer what they need.

What Makes a First Mover?

There is a saying that "all politics are local." It's fair to say that all business is local, too. It's the people and groups you meet in the evolving communities that will lead you to new business possibilities. Belonging to these groups, networking with the participants, and monitoring present activities and future trends for your industry is the personal side of a global business. Corporations spend millions to establish worldwide sales forces. But the sales themselves are conducted one-on-one. People meet, get to know one another, and solve the problems of other people.

You may not have millions to invest to grab a new market niche. But you become a first mover by association when you participate in the efforts that launch a user community. At that point, you are entrenched. You have an in, and you force your challengers to come to you. You occupy the playing field and learn its nuances. That doesn't mean you can't be displaced, but your challengers must work harder to displace you than you must work to remain where you are. It is no different on the Internet than anywhere else, even if meetings are not held face-to-face.

But what the Internet does support is communities with no geographic location, bound only by a common need for information, resources, and a common currency. The Internet enables casual conversations to grow into full-blown industries, complete with conventions and trade magazines. It's just a matter of applying the proper tools. Such tools are easy to find. Net-based businesses can provide everything from hosting space and site development, to product management, to online ordering and fulfillment. Those skilled in low-cost market dynamics build the community and bring the challenger to an already established space. They do not arrive at another's space and become the challenger, looking to conquer that space.

But what if your opponent won't come to the battle? What if they are happy building their own community? Perhaps it's a slightly different niche, but one that still competes with you for physical

177

resources, employees, and customers. In such a case, your competition will be happy to remain where he is and grow strong, while you attempt to do the same. Then, as each of you grow, a battle looms because of the need for expansion. In such cases, it may be in your best interest to hasten a direct challenge. On your terms, of course.

To win this way, you must draw the competitor into a battle you can win on a field you control. It is difficult, of course, to force someone to you under such circumstances. But you can draw them in by appearing to offer some advantage. Only do so if the time is right. If the time is not right, you can keep the opponent at bay without actually fighting until you choose the time.

In a traditional war, Sun Tzu says, generals will judge the enemy and use their situation against them. When enemy troops are at ease, he works to tire them, when they are well fed, he works to starve them, when they are at rest, he makes them move. He will enact quick attacks at places the enemy is unable to rescue, or move swiftly toward places where he is least expected, causing the enemy to react or even retreat.

And when you do move, go where there is no opponent, and occupy that area, market space, or product idea. Moving this way creates fewer expenses, and less wear and tear on your organization. To be certain that you capture an area, take one that has no established multitude. Your opponent cannot defend a place it does not occupy. If the opponent wants the space you have taken, it will have to battle much harder to achieve it. Its extended development and marketing efforts will be taxing.

You are always able to hold the space you have occupied when your opponent is unable to attack, or dares not try, if you are skilled at protecting your market and your customer relationships. If the service you provide is so valued that undercutting your product price doesn't matter, then your opponent will not know what to attack. Likewise, if you are skilled in attacking, your opponent will not know what to defend. You can catch him off guard. Or simply leave him guessing and using up valuable resources as he tries to prepare for you.

If you become expert at this game—capturing new business, defending your new ground, and then capturing more—your enemy will need to work harder to understand you, your motives, and your business plan.

Stealth should be your rule. You should be like an announced merger that seems to come out of nowhere, or an IPO that runs wild on its first day, leaving many would-be investors cursing their lack of knowledge. Your secrecy is your strength as you grow. A true expert leaves no trace of his intentions. Give no advanced warning. The expert becomes the master—you become the master—of your enemy's fate not by controlling the enemy, but by denying them the ability to understand and react to you.

When the time comes to fight for the position you need, make your organization and your efforts invincible by focusing on your enemy's weak positions. **There is always the temptation to focus a knockout blow on the strongest assets. But attacking the opponent at a strong point will cost you more time and resources, without the promise of a clear victory.** It is best to move toward the opponent's weakest points. You will be victorious. Your opponent must then give up small pieces of business as you advance, or expend considerable energy protecting a market space that isn't vital to its business and slowly defeat itself.

Even a firmly entrenched company with a multimillion-dollar business must either relinquish those small chunks of business or work ceaselessly to engage and compete with a smaller company. The choice is tough because the larger company realizes the smaller company chose to attack an area where it knows it can win. The larger company must decide if a defense effort is worth the cost, given the marginal nature of the business being grabbed.

The Other Low-Hanging Fruit

There is another way, though the payoff may not be as lucrative. That's to look for firmly established niches that are not particularly lucrative at the moment, but which have potential. Those are the markets to carefully analyze. Someone else may have been first mover, but if the niche is not particularly profitable, they may not have staying power. If you analyze market growth, dollars spent, and expansion possibilities for the niche, you may decide it's worth your while simply to buy your way in.

Around 1980, a company called Seattle Computer developed one of the first personal computer operating systems called QDOS (for Quick and Dirty Operating System). This was a very niche-market product designed to run on the company's line of 8086 microcomputers. Future growth possibilities were not clear.

At the same time, Microsoft was a small company marketing a computer-language product called Microsoft Basic. It was looking to expand into the operating system business. Microsoft made a rapid entry into this niche simply by licensing QDOS and reworking it. Then, Microsoft licensed the new version to IBM for use on the IBM PC, and an empire was born. All it took was a simple buy-in to a niche product right before its market exploded.

Not exploiting new market niches may create big problems if niches grow. Consider the plight of poor Kodak. The Rochester, New York, monolith was synonymous with quality photo products for years. But the digital revolution struck right at the heart of the company. Digital cameras are wonderful things, but can you imagine being in a situation where your core product, film, may no longer be necessary? Yes, it will be a slow decline, and for many applications, there is no substitute for film. But Kodak's bread and butter is the family snapshot, and when mom and dad switch to digital cameras, the effect is shattering.

With occasional spikes and dips, Kodak's stock price mostly hovered between 60 and 80 for five years. But in fall 2000, it dropped into the 30s. Besides the threat to its core film product, there's also the issue of photo paper and how people now share photos. Many share digital images over the Web instead of making extra copies. And they can duplicate the digital image as many times as they want.

How can Kodak survive this kind of hit? The company will survive, most likely by realizing that the Internet brings opportunities along with this new type of battle. Kodak will need to partner with multiple other businesses in order to survive. Kodak CEO Dan Carp has outlined some of the ways the old Kodak will migrate to the new.

In the old days, people snapped photos, sent them to a developer, and then received their developed prints. The new method involves multiple input and output devices, many of which do not include Kodak. But, eventually, such images will need to have a high-quality output, or they will need to be manipulated. For example, a digital camera takes a picture. From there, it can be posted to a Web page, pressed into a CD-ROM, or sent to an Internet-connected TV set. Along the way, software is used to reduce or enlarge, change the format for multiple uses, and display the image in multiple ways. Again, some of that software will be Kodak's, and some will not. Perhaps you'll have a far different sort of desktop printer than you do now that can print a photo on Kodak paper. Perhaps you will display rotating images in a high-quality Kodak LCD photo frame (prototypes are available now). Perhaps the image will be compressed and stored in Kodak-managed photo libraries or faxed to others and viewed in a Kodak fax viewer.

Kodak's ventures into digital imaging have been marginally successful in the past. But now, it is aiming at still-developing market spaces rather than playing catch-up, which provides a better chance for succeeding. It's a great example of an old company adapting to a new situation, capitalizing on the very technologies that threaten to put it out of business.

Established businesses that have fought a few battles should be good at this, as long as they remember how modern Internet marketplaces differ from the markets and battles of old.

- **In traditional battle, space is finite. Countries went to war over assets like access to certain ports, farmland, or mineral-rich mountains. On the Internet, space is practically infinite.** New market spaces can be constructed anywhere. Yes, there is an advantage in being associated with the top online portals. But the potential to build your own exists if you can't come to terms with current leaders.

• **In ancient times, city-states mostly spent money to protect places where they had an economic interest. They might venture out to protect other areas, simply to keep their chief rivals from gaining a foothold there. But logistics for such operations could be daunting.** Without a direct benefit, it was tough to keep such an operation going for very long. Today, the largest companies may choose to dump unfathomable amounts of money into new markets just to keep rivals from winning those spaces. Consider Microsoft's reaction to Netscape as Netscape began capturing the evolving new market for Web browsers. Netscape entered that battlefield first. It entrenched itself. It held the lead even as Microsoft attacked by introducing its own Internet Explorer (IE) Web browser.

Microsoft lost a big opportunity to be first mover for a very important market. But Microsoft's size gave it a fantastic tactical advantage as it struggled to catch up. In this case, Microsoft did two things that made it very difficult for Netscape to compete. It announced it would no longer charge money for IE, and it started bundling the browser with its operating system. Millions of new machines came with Microsoft Windows and IE pre-installed. Netscape lost market share quickly, falling from about 97 percent of the browser market in 1995, to about 15 percent by the end of 2000.

Another part of Microsoft's strategy to make IE the world's browsing standard was to integrate it so tightly that it became difficult for Microsoft Windows users to switch from IE. Hyperlinks could be embedded in spreadsheet and word documents, launching the browser when they were clicked. The company faced severe legal challenges for this, but the effort was successful. The overall investment Microsoft made to win this space went far beyond what most companies would invest without a revenue stream. But Microsoft knew it had to remain the dominant player as the focus moved from PCs to the Net itself.

Today, IE remains a free product, and Microsoft owns a jewel of a market space because of its effort.

Netscape retaliated in some interesting ways. It also eliminated the fee for its browser, but it lacked the huge distribution engine Microsoft enjoyed. Thus, Netscape found no strategic advantage in that tactic. Instead, Netscape now focuses on offering its product across multiple platforms—as many as 33 different machines and configurations. Its main browser package is Netscape Communicator, which combines the browser with several other features, including e-mail. In 1998, Netscape released Communicator's source code to the public. This is basically machine instructions in their original form before they are compiled to run on various machines. Programmers need the source code to modify a program. Making it public allows other developers to make improvements and additions to the software. By the time Netscape released Netscape 6 in fall 2000, it began moving aggressively into Extensible Markup Language (XML) support and into an environment where the browser software can easily be repurposed, slimmed down, or changed for use on a variety of devices.

Regardless of Netscape's first-to-market positioning, irrespective of its great market share and defensive positioning, Microsoft wore Netscape down and eventually captured the majority of the browser market by spending the time, money, and energy necessary to steal a product from the market leader. Netscape answered by heading off in a slightly different direction, extending the type of people and type of machines it could serve. Should Microsoft be slow to adapt to future shifts in browser technologies or market needs, it's possible that Netscape could again find itself in a leading position.

Had Microsoft arrived in the browser space first, had it worked to develop the market instead of watching it rise out of the University of Illinois (under that original name Mosaic), it's likely that its effort to win would not have been nearly as expensive or complex. It's also unlikely that Microsoft would have given its browser away for free. It would not have sacrificed so heavily to catch up and overtake a new competitor. It should have known the disposition of this potential competitor before it emerged with a spectacular product.

A good leader will work to determine the enemy's dispositions while concealing her own. This lets you concentrate on a defined purpose and plan, while your enemies must divide their efforts in anticipation of your possible actions. When such a division occurs, you can then use your entire strength to attack just a fraction of your opponent's force.

Microsoft had to play catch-up because it never saw Mosaic coming. The product exploded before anyone realized how fast the technology was falling together.

There are two parts to this lesson—Microsoft's mistake and Netscape's mistake. In the early 1990s, the Internet was fragmented. Connections to servers were made via different protocols and client software. Graphics were viewed with separate viewing tools. Finding anything was difficult, and rudimentary navigation tools like Archie or Gopher were unreliable. Many people realized a universal navigation tool that showed text, images, and hyperlinks in the same window would be a killer application. Microsoft likely could have built such a browser first, had it realized the intense public desire for this tool.

From Netscape's standpoint, it's a harsh lesson on the necessity to know your adversary's resources before developing your business plan. **What happens when you are first mover, but are then cut off by a competitor who can outspend you? Do you have a second path in mind, like Netscape's open-source efforts, that might keep you alive?**

Consider another Microsoft example. In March 2000, Microsoft purchased 20 percent of RealNames. This was a key indication that Microsoft views America Online as its archenemy on the Internet. Why? Because it showed that Microsoft decided to seriously target one of the primary technologies that helped its growing rival deliver an easy interface to its users. AOL uses keywords to help people navigate. Enter a keyword, and go to a specific spot. RealNames delivered that same power to the Microsoft's IE. It's not the first battle between AOL and Microsoft. In 1999, the two also fought over instant-messaging technology and market share for that utility.

When Microsoft isn't first mover, the Redmond, Washington, company seems to have a specific tactic for displacing the leader. Microsoft identifies the leader in a key field, creates a similar product, and pulls customers away from the competitor through its marketing muscle and by associating or distributing the new product along with its omnipresent Windows operating system. This technique helped Microsoft siphon business away from IBM, Apple, and the PC market in general.

The technique works on two levels. It helps a company like Microsoft quickly establish a product for a known market. And if played correctly, it slows the growth of the competing product. This is an important lesson for anyone who wants to avoid the risks of being a first mover, waiting instead to later steal business from the first mover after the viability of the niche is clear.

But how do you start siphoning off business if you can't afford to give your product away? One ploy is to position your challenging technology as an open standard that anyone in the marketplace can use. It's what Netscape did to compete with Microsoft. It's what Microsoft did to compete with AOL (AOL's keyword feature is used on its proprietary subscription service, and IE is publicly available). With Microsoft backing the RealNames standard, the upstart could become the dominant technology. People would expect to see this Web-wide functionality on AOL, too, and it could be very costly for AOL to translate its keyword system into the Microsoft mold.

So here are the basics.

• **If you own a proprietary technology that makes you the dominant player in your field, leverage it hard and grow your market share. People will criticize your proprietary system and then attack you with open standards.**

• **If you don't own the proprietary technology, and you see a market that you want a piece of, try to level the playing field. Work the other side of the equation and create or support an open technology that does the same thing as the market leader.** Work in loose alliances with other companies to promote the technology as the better solution. Build a user base that supports the open technology as an alternative. Then start competing for your share of the new user base. Your size and ability to innovate will determine your success in this type of play.

185

- **As you gain market share, pull away and differentiate your product as the new leader, even though it's based on open standards.** If you win, the process begins again as others challenge your leadership.

Intimate Strangers

When you battle head-to-head with a competitor for the same Internet market space, each of you must anticipate the other's moves. Where will your business evolve? Where will theirs? Will you pursue expensive, high-profile marketing or take the viral path, letting word-of-mouth drive your success? Will you buy people or full companies to get the talent and technologies you need? Will either you or your opponent make an exclusive deal for a technology that the other can't live without? Perhaps they will anticipate your moves but spread too thin attempting to answer them. You will choose which strengths of yours, and weaknesses of theirs, to exploit.

Doing that helps you successfully divide your opponent. Then you alone choose your plan of attack. Even if the other company is vast and their employees talented, you will be superior numerically, and your strategy will be intensely focused because you are concentrating on just one thing, while they have many things to contend with. You will have the resources to do a better job.

The other guy or the other business must never know where you intend to concentrate your business efforts. Lacking such knowledge, the opponent must prepare in a great many places. Too many places. Resources are diluted. Product efforts are wasted. And you will meet little resistance in the marketplace because the other company's response will be weak.

Think of how your competitor might react if she knew you reduced your number of product development people and increased your outside sales staff? What if that change was made in time for the fall conference season, when your sales staffers could target more people to visit and more deals to sign? What if your competitor wasn't sure what kind of wireless protocol and strategy you planned to pursue, and decided to pursue several strategies to be sure your challenge was met? Would your competitor be spread too thin? Would you take advantage of this if you knew it?

You will strike at a few selected points, and claim specific business. Some may not even be what you intended to claim. They are just opportunities that presented themselves, and you followed them.

> **In a classic battle situation, Sun Tzu says, "If he prepares to the front, his rear will be weak, and if to the rear, his front will be fragile. If he strengthens his left, his right will be vulnerable, and if his right, there will be few troops on his left. And when he sends troops everywhere, he will be weak everywhere. Numerical weakness comes from having to guard against possible attacks; numerical strength from forcing the enemy to make these preparations against us."**

In many ways, this is how smaller sites manage to steal traffic away from big portal sites. "We focus on one thing and do it well, they don't," said one developer of kids' Web sites and filtering services. "We may only have a handful of engineers, but they're all focused on building a couple of products. The big portals are busy trying to be all things to all people. They have more engineers, but they really don't have more engineers to focus on one product like we do. How could we not be better?"

The more widely you can separate your opponent's workers on multiple projects, the more you dilute your opponent's ability to respond.

In World War II, the Allies had one major advantage over Germany as they prepared for the inevitable and horrible D-Day invasion that loomed in their future. The Allies knew when and where the invasion would occur. The Germans in occupied France didn't have that luxury. They had a rough idea. The Allied forces had to cross the English Channel. But there is a lot of French coastline along the channel. German soldiers were spread over hundreds of miles to ensure that it was protected. Shifts had to stay on alert 24 hours a day. Even with that uncertainty, it was hard enough for the Allies to fight their way ashore on beaches we now know by their code names, like Omaha and Utah. If the Germans had known precisely where Omaha and Utah were located, D-Day might have a far different history. It would be a story of Allied losses and failure, and German victory.

Without knowing the battleground, and without possessing a time, the opponent is at a disadvantage. With that knowledge, the defender becomes a surprisingly powerful foe.

The Consolidation Conundrum

Surviving industry consolidation in a contracting market is different from fighting for market share in an expanding market. When markets consolidate, cooperation with a former competitor can be just as important as beating them, especially if they have something you need in order to survive.

In summer 2000, the popular online computer-information site CNET merged with the massive computer magazine group Ziff-Davis. Some pundits argued that both offer nearly identical news and tech information. Why did they need each other? But CNET didn't just eliminate its biggest competitor when it bought Ziff. It also bought reach. While Ziff's content was similar, it offered the potential of nearly doubling CNET's core audience, potentially pushing it to the number seven spot at the time in Media Metrix's Web survey of top traffic sites. That's a mighty big plum to pick when everyone else is collapsing. When market consolidation happens, it's important to turn an evaluating eye to competitors. Not necessarily to defeat them, but to figure out whom you might work with.

• **Establish a benchmark by which you judge other companies.** It's a comparative standard to help you judge what is fair and what constitutes a good deal when interacting with other companies. If you feel the other side is using a benchmark that is unfair to you (such as requiring an open standard you don't support or a defined technology different from yours), work with them to introduce a new benchmark. For example, people constantly challenge the federal government when it sends out requests for proposals when it wants to buy Windows computers. If you're a Unix vendor, you know you'll only make a sale if you change the benchmark used in the RFP.

• **Realize that it may be tough to convince a competitor to give you all his business, or to sell you her entire company.** Try instead to get your foot in the door with a limited partnership. Then look for clues. Are other suppliers or partners not doing well? Can you move in to acquire that share of the business? Surpass the potential partner's expectations, and your role will expand.

• **Some negotiators believe you should always pressure the other side to give in first.** But sometimes it's better to be the first to concede when you negotiate. It may put you in a position of strength. You are not the bad guy. You have shown you can compromise. Now it's their turn. (Just make your concession minimal, and hold fast until you receive something in return.)

• **Be an expert.** Sell your expertise, experience, and track record. Emphasize the special qualities of your business. Are you a rare commodity with a distinct value that can be leveraged? Do not be arrogant. Let the record alone speak for you. Others are searching desperately for something to cling to when an industry shakeout is under way. If you look successful, those who feel danger will turn to you to help them survive.

• **Whom do the executives you want to partner with admire?** Perhaps you can emulate them, or even tie your business to them somehow. Others will follow you because of your proximity to the admired person.

It's All about Focus; It's All about Change

The game extends to competitive marketing, too. Editors for large trade magazines often receive 200 pieces of regular mail per day, plus hundreds of e-mails. These include oceans of cookie-cutter press releases meant to announce varying levels of breakthroughs for new products and technologies. One thing an editor quickly learns is that some companies send out far too many press releases. They don't concentrate on the important events for their company. What happens then is the company's truly important news gets lost in the noise. A wise company will always have a story or quote ready for a reporter who needs it, but they save their big pitches for the proper time. Partnerships, buyouts, and mergers make some of the best press releases.

Some companies, or industry groups, also know the art of diluting other companies' announcements. For example, if one computer company announces machines with the fastest microprocessors ever, then a rival microprocessor company issues, on the same day, an announcement of lab tests for their new processor that's twice as fast.

It doesn't matter that the chip won't go into production for several months, the announcement is made and it has a diluting effect on the first company's announcement. If they are lucky, the second company will ride the first one's coattails, getting a mention in a round-up story about microprocessors, effectively making their announcement look as important as the other.

The first chip manufacturer should have avoided leaks, broad pre-announcements, and such so that the second company could not steal its thunder. (Preannouncements to a few key press people are still fine.)

Keep your marketing efforts secret. At the same time, analyze an opponent's plans. Any shortcomings you see will become your strong points.

Like the Soviet border flights discussed in a previous chapter, you can prod or agitate competing businesses to discover the pattern of their movements. How do they react when you show up at the same trade shows? Do you talk to the same trade press or develop similar products? Are they slow or quick to respond? Do you have the tools and the people to capture the business that your opponent is underserving?

Remain liquid. You can change. You have to change, based on what your enemy does. There is a Dilbert comic strip in which the pointy-haired boss says the company's strategic plan is to research what competitors are doing and react to that. Dilbert responds that's the same as having no strategy. But Dilbert is only partially correct. From a product development and marketing standpoint, reaction isn't really a plan. But as a leader, behind closed doors, you know that reacting to change is very much part of the plan. It is your ability to adjust that will keep your company alive, while you are looking like a steadfast stay-the-course sort of leader. (And woe to you if, instead, you look more like the pointy-haired boss.)

Have no ascertainable shape. Your opponent's research team, even spies if they are sent, will not discern what your plans are. And then your opponent can't lay plans against you. If your opponent does strike out, you absorb the punch like water that flows around the fist.

> **Sun Tzu says, "It is according to the situations that plans are laid for victory, but the multitude does not comprehend this. Although everyone can see the outward aspects, none understands how the victory is achieved."**

Yes, an army plans, but it manages its victory in accordance with the situation of the enemy. An important point to remaining liquid is to not repeat the same actions for every partnership and project.

An Internet business of course makes plans, but it manages its products and progress in accordance with a volatile marketplace. It also must judge what an ever-shifting opponent is capable of. There are no constant conditions. There should be no permanent solutions or battle plan. Nowhere is that more apparent than in the 20-minutes-from-now world of the Net.

"Therefore, when a victory is won, one's tactics are not repeated. One should always respond to circumstances in an infinite variety of ways."

Ask yourself, did your big press tour work well last time? Then, this time, invite the press to a two-day conference at a swank hotel. Did you spend last year developing big, stand-alone products? Then spend this year arranging those products into vertical channels, filling in gaps as you provide integrated solutions.

Water flows. It avoids blockages. It avoids fights and takes multiple paths. You also need to flow, around the blocks, past the heights, and into the low areas, filling and changing. All this happens while your increasingly competitive company avoids challenges and strikes at your opponent's weaknesses.

In business, there are no constant conditions. One who is able to win the victory by modifying his tactics in accordance with the enemy has a great advantage. Of the five elements that Sun Tzu draws upon [water, fire, metal, wood, and earth], he knew none is always pre-dominant; of the four seasons, none lasts forever; of the days, some are long and some short, and the moon waxes and wanes. These variations establish a normal and successful rhythm.

It is up to you to fall into such a rhythm, and exploit your advantage every time your wave crests.

hit moving targets

earlier we learned that middlemen who improve access will be the only middlemen who survive. But that doesn't mean they will survive every round of disintermediation. Thus, you have to look as far down the road as possible to see where your target market is heading.

Let's say you've built a successful Web site that tells car owners how to spot trouble in their vehicles, plus information on how to fix such problems and where to take their cars for service. How will such a site survive when more cars are fitted with wireless Internet connections? The computer under the car's hood will analyze the engine and directly check the manufacturer's database to know when performance is lagging. This technology advance connects two people: (1) the car owner, who may or may not want to get involved in the car's maintenance and (2) the auto manufacturer's Web site. The Web site still offers a great service, but when the car itself can investigate its own service requirements, the site becomes a middleman that can be bypassed.

If you don't enhance access, you are part of the problem, and you will not be part of any new solution.

The march is constant. Further in the future, even the under-hood computer could be disintermediated by an even better advance. But ever-newer business opportunities open each time others close.

Some of the most successful e-commerce companies today have not necessarily excelled at disintermediating, or improving efficiency. This raises questions about their long-term viability.

For example, Amazon.com has always operated its own warehouses and shipping services. In the late 1990s, the company bought four new mammoth warehouses in what founder Jeff Bezos described as the "fastest expansion in distribution capacity in peacetime history." The effort was understandable, but not necessarily wise. One of the main reasons customers reject an e-commerce site (besides confusion over a user interface) is when the item they want is out of stock. By tightly controlling its own inventory, Amazon could make sure no one would leave because an item was unavailable.

But owning warehouses, staffing them, holding idle inventory, and handling shipping adds to a company's costs, and Amazon is in a low-margin business. Even though it's one of the Net's top retailers, Amazon has bled red ink through the late 1990s and into the new century. Luckily, investors love Amazon because it's a market leader, and because it's aggressively taken investments in some of the companies it deals with. But a basic question lingers about how Amazon can handle so much of its operation itself.

"I think that's a suspect strategy because the competencies required to manage a logistics business are entirely orthogonal to the competencies required to run a .com business," said Lycos's Sege. "Logistics is all about getting the planes to run on time and managing the forklifts and warehouses, managing the square footage and hourly workers. Managing a .com company is all about promotion and marketing and database management and building efficient IT infrastructure. There is little in common between the two. Having one executive who believes he can be adept at both is difficult. Plus, the world of logistics is already populated by people who do this very well. Unless you think you can do the job better than Roadway, UPS, DHL, or FedEx, my notion is that you should leave your logistics piece to those guys, and focus on building a great e-tailer. Then cut a deal where it's win-win for both the logistics expert and you."

Compare the Amazon model to the Garden.com model. In many ways, Garden followed the design of old mail-order seed catalogs, except that its catalog is online. But Garden.com operated no central warehouse. This is wise, since it also offers live plants, which are costly to keep. Instead, it followed the old drop-ship method, in which a store takes an order, but allows the manufacturer (or grower in this case) to ship the order.

Garden.com had a front-end Web site and a back-end commerce system that moves order information to its suppliers, who handle shipments. The Austin, Texas, company had a small warehouse that handles gift items, but its suppliers carry most of the product inventory and absorb those associated costs and risks. Yet, the suppliers seem happy with the arrangement. Some of them are wholesale farms and greenhouses who view Garden.com as a way to expand their business as they'd never be able to build themselves.

To handle the information flow, Garden.com developed with FedEx a proprietary system called Trellis. It's a Web-centric system housed on a cluster of Sun Solaris application servers. It uses the Java 2 Enterprise Edition (J2EE) architecture that allows new plug-and-play components to be added. Beyond an order-taking system, Trellis attempts to serve as a full supply chain solution. Suppliers can plug into the system quickly and obtain the information they need to manage their own piece of the business. For example, both suppliers and customers have real-time visibility, via FedEx, on the status of every order. Several suppliers also use bar codes on all items to update inventory data and confirm that selected items match an order.

Some Garden.com suppliers have even shared best-practice suggestions for operations and shipping with other suppliers, feeling that the overall success of Garden.com would help everyone's business.

Studies have shown that the costs of goods sold in a virtual enterprise relying on drop-shipped orders are roughly the same as in a traditional system. Shipping costs are actually higher, since items are handled individually and usually shipped overnight. But inventory carrying costs are much lower. So is order fulfillment.

Imagine how Amazon could cut costs if it processed orders, but allowed the publisher of an ordered book to ship it directly. Amazon might give up some control, but it might also be able to eliminate warehouses and staff.

Unfortunately, Garden.com had a great idea, but ramping up was costly, and turning a profit quickly was difficult. The company burned through about $63 million between 1998 and 2000. In September 2000, it announced layoffs and a restructuring, and an autumn audit by Ernst & Young raised "substantial doubt" that it could continue absorbing losses as it grew. By Christmas 2000, Garden.com filled its last orders and shut its doors.

On the face of things, Amazon, even with its more costly model, was more successful than Garden.com. The question is, Which is the model for the future? Garden.com may or may not survive for the long term. But its concept for how an Internet sales operation should be managed seems sound enough that the Altee Burpee Company, the famous seed catalog company, acquired Garden.com to keep the idea going.

To remain competitive in such shifting landscapes, leaders need to have a strong sense of technology change and business savvy. As long as they keep in mind that the magical access is the driving force for online change, it should be easier for them to see which changes are important, and which will not make a major long-term impact.

Search engines became the major portals to the Internet because they help people find information. Web auction sites found success because they help collectors and bargain hunters find items they couldn't locate in their own neighborhoods. But what is the future for businesses like online bill paying services or real-estate offices that force customers to sign up for site access, and then show only houses in their own listings? Will they be disintermediated in the years ahead?

Attempts at consolidation and disintermediation can have mixed consequences. The huge food company General Mills worked with Empriva Technologies to develop a system that allowed managers across the company to check on things as simple as where an order for a box of cereal was in the company system. Previously, such an order moved across about 10 different computer systems, and no one had a single view of an order's progress. Such a system helps purchasing managers view the total process so they can start squeezing out inefficiencies and saving money.

Beyond internal systems, General Mills is working with other consumer product companies like Pillsbury, Coca-Cola, PepsiCo, and Hershey Foods to initiate Transora, a global consumer goods marketplace where purchasing managers can buy large quantities of items and find distribution mechanisms.

Some key industry players creating large purchasing exchanges are:

- Covisint (auto parts) by Ford, General Motors, and Daimler-Chrysler

- Quadrem (metals and minerals) by Alcoa, BHP, Alcan Aluminum, and others

- Pantelos (energy exchange) by PG&E, Consolidated Edison, and Entergy

- AirNewCo (aviation) by American, Continental, Delta, and United Airlines

- E2Open (electronics) by Nortel Networks, IBM, Toshiba, and Solectron

These exchanges allow corporations who purchase huge quantities of parts, services, or consumables to aggregate their procurement for better pricing. They also allow new companies to reach these key purchasers and get into the game. It remains to be seen if these huge exchanges will encounter any regulatory problems down the road, because when so many companies work together, the potential for price fixing and market manipulation rises.

Still, when we talk about winning market share, we're talking about winning access to communities and customers, who then use your services so much that you become the de facto winner of that market niche. Large exchanges are a way for the producer and the consumer to find that access.

Once that user base is established, things like computing power, connections, the people who make up the Net, and the vast databases connected to the Net become important, because those are the aspects people want to access. Each has a supply and demand economy of its own.

The Leader's Role

It is the role of the leader to understand the push and pull of market forces that affect a business, and to coordinate how the company will react to them.

In war, a general receives his commands from the king, the president, or some other head of state. In a public company, a chief executive officer is usually trusted to make decisions on her own, but a board of directors is always watching closely and raising important questions.

The people attempting to influence the CEO will not always know all the other forces tugging and influencing his business decisions. Many will second-guess some decisions because they may focus on the next quarter rather than three years down the road. Yet just like a general who must deal with state intrusions that complicate the mission, a

CEO has to deal with those who do not understand the small and large supply and demand issues that influence daily choices.

Thus, when rolling out a large-scale development effort, the leader's main task is to establish a responsible reporting structure that provides both an accurate view of what's happening in the organization, and a mechanism by which changes and a refocusing of efforts can be carried out. It is an upstream and downstream flow. Most growing organizations have one of these parts in place. The most successful have both.

Assembling a team and mobilizing that team for the task at hand is the most difficult part of any battle. There is nothing more difficult in this world than establishing a process to assure that all parts of a project are developed in concert, that the pieces will fall together at the proper times (and fit), that deadlines will be met and costs will be contained.

It is far more likely that schedules will fall out of sync. Software will be incompatible. Items delivered will not be to spec, or different teams will have a different idea about what the spec is. Costs will rise as changes are made to get everything back into sync.

It is the project and product managers who put the pieces together for your organization. They are the captains and majors who execute the plans developed by others. They are the overseers who make sure the work gets done, and the first ones to notice when things fall out of place. Tracking their progress via reports is extremely important for keeping a company on track. If a project starts falling behind, and the product or project managers are not elevating issues to their leaders, it may be that they are not doing their jobs. Fighting the chaos, solving small problems, and elevating larger problems until a solution is found *is* their job.

Therefore, leaders must assemble a work team and mobilize their people, blending them into a harmonious entity that works well together, yet which can adjust as needed. It's a difficult task, and only half your employees will ever fall into this mode. Strip out the dead wood as needed. An organization that knows how to maneuver for advantageous market positions without slowing down any of the work it is already doing will ultimately be successful.

In some ways, this makes a business leader's job tougher than that of a traditional general in command of an army. A general also knows the value of stealth, and stealth is his command. But a director of a developing organization is often forced to tip her hand as she seeks employees, money, and partners.

Stealth, Deception, and Secrecy— The Opposite of Access?

If access to products and information is key to growth, keeping such information quiet as you develop your business plan is equally important.

Previous chapters outline the need for you to be a stealthy organization. **Your challenge is to make sure that your devious route is also the most direct route.** You need to get from point A to point B, and you need to get there fast. Yet you don't want to be noticed going after a particular market space or type of business before you are able to capture it.

> **It** is a paradox. You want a market space. You don't want people to know you want it.

Imagine going before an investment capital firm to outline your business plan, but saying that you can't tell them everything about your plan because it's a strategic secret. You'd be shown the door faster than a trench coat–wearing party crasher at a sweet-16 party.

Or imagine trying to hire the best people without telling them what market you are targeting and what you hope to do. You may get some employees—probably the type who just want a job and don't care what it is. You won't get the most ambitious people with the best skills.

> **The** trick is to move secretly, yet share enough information to start the process rolling, so that people know you are serious and that you are on an important mission.

200

Beyond stealth, you may also notice that you are headed into conflict with another company. At that point, you will need to redirect your opponent so her efforts are focused elsewhere, or you may need to adjust your own plans. It's a delicate dance of adjustment and one-upmanship.

In the last chapter, we stress the importance of getting to the battlefield first to capture new markets, technologies, and business. By diverting your opponent, you assure that you *do* get to the evolving market first because your opponent will be elsewhere. (Outright misrepresentation is frowned on though, so be sure you do this without running afoul of the Federal Trade Commission laws.)

Here's one example of two rivals outmaneuvering each other to gain market share and recognition, while shifting focus along the way to expand their business in new ways. Corbis and Getty Images are two huge digital image archives that have conducted a breakneck acquisition spree trying to outpace one another. Each has attempted to create the largest, most profitable collection of digitized photos, paintings, posters, and more.

The move toward online digital image archives is interesting. Traditionally, people who need a specific photograph for a magazine story, book, or ad campaign scour glossy printed books issued by commercial photo libraries. When a photo is located with just the right look to illustrate a point, a license is purchased, and a transparency is sent from the photo library. But this process is expensive and time-consuming. The books have to be designed and printed. Buyers have to flip through them, and the ordering and delivery process is awkward.

With digital photo archives, visitors can search by keyword like football or sunshine, or by a concept like winning or celebrate. Thumbnail images are displayed. Low-resolution images can be viewed immediately. High-resolution images for commercial use can be purchased and downloaded.

Corbis started establishing its position by the mid-1990s. But Getty made fast strategic moves. In 1998, Getty completed a $200 million merger with PhotoDisc, a player in the royalty-free photo market (pay once for unlimited use). Corbis answered this move by making its own play for the royalty-free space, buying Digital Stock for an undisclosed sum. That helped Corbis establish its online print and poster shop, which sells posters reprinted from Digital Stock images.

Getty then added the Allsport sports photo agency to its archive, for $27 million plus over a million shares of stock. This gave the company hundreds of thousands of more images from high-visibility sport events, including the Olympics.

Rather than concentrate immediately on one-upmanship, Corbis started investing heavily in its infrastructure, developing the database and e-comm pieces for storing, selling, and delivering high-res images. At a certain point, Corbis managers realized that the size of an archive would become less important than finding pictures in all that noise, and delivering them easily.

Because high-bandwidth connections are still a problem at some small shops, Corbis also moved into the CD-ROM business, pressing and delivering images on disk by overnight mail. At the end of 2000, Corbis and Getty were the two main players in the digital image business, controlling about 45 percent of all available digitized images.

Corbis has the name recognition. It's owned by Microsoft's Bill Gates and offers 65 million images (many of them famous). About 8 percent of those images were available online by the end of 2000. Corbis Images is the licensing division that targets creative professionals who desire commercial use of an image, while Corbis.com is an Internet image archive for consumers. You can find everything from Ansel Adams prints to van Gogh screen savers via Corbis, but its main business is selling striking photos used in the media.

Getty Images, owned by oil heir Mark Getty, maintains a collection of 70 million images. The Getty site is not as easy to browse as Corbis, since its images are segmented in different collections, and its search tools are not robust. But it seems that Getty has a lead not only in the size, but also in the value of its collection. Its acquisition of Art.com was a powerful strategic move. Currently, Corbis appears stronger in news and editorial images while Getty is stronger in advertising images, which tend to generate more money. As each collection grew with more acquisitions, the companies specifically took different roads, often reacting to the other's moves.

Getty branched into stock video and music. Corbis bought Saba, a privately held photo agency with a strong international presence. Getty started licensing and distributing its content through other sites, like Lycos and ZDNet. Corbis made it easy to browse and download low-resolution images from its site, essentially making it a popular stop for students researching papers and amateur artists. It also added great browsing and photo descriptions.

Getty maneuvered with powerful new deals, such as an exclusive deal to feature National Geographic content and an agreement with Ofoto, an Internet photo company, for custom high-quality photographic printing services. Corbis may have arrived at this battlefield first, but Getty pushed in hard and created new opportunities and effectively expanded the market as it went.

Playing both sides against the middle, Ofoto also struck a deal with Corbis. "It can be difficult working with both because they are very passionate competitors," said James Joaquin, president and CEO of Ofoto. "Everyone tried to sign us to an exclusive. But we have to be Switzerland in our business. We need to be able to scale our print volume as high as possible for as many partners as possible." It's always a good move to not tie your future too closely to one other company.

The evolution of these two companies is a powerful study of action and reaction that produced no clear winners. In this case, the companies quietly maneuvered and surprised each other. In traditional warfare, opposing sides try to create diversions and roadblocks to slow the other side, hoping to reach the battlefield first.

Sun Tzu tells us that an army that takes the proper defense posture can never be defeated, and an army that waits until the time is right to attack can never lose. When we look at Corbis and Getty, we can only surmise that the time has not yet come that will produce a clear victory for either. Or it may be that the market is big enough for both. Remember, any business can be broken into its supply chain components and structured as a JIT operation if it has good information flow. For example, Getty's Art.com sells a lot of consumer prints for home or office decorations. Ofoto offers the print-on-demand solution. When you have 20 million digitized images, you want to sell to consumers. You can't print 20 million copies and hold them in a warehouse. You need a solution so that when the customer orders, the print is printed out just for that order.

You'd think a company like Ofoto would itself be an acquisition target by the two competitive image companies, but it's likely that Corbis and Getty will continue to concentrate on image acquiring and licensing images and not on becoming service industries. Ofoto's main threat is from similar service providers like Shutterfly and Photoworks.

If you can become an artist at using tactics to stall, mislead, and misinform, you will have a better chance of distracting your opponent and assuring that the space you want is not occupied. Within your own company, if you are maneuvering for a plum assignment, you can tell others how thankless the task will be while you stay up late creating a PowerPoint presentation explaining to your superiors how you will accomplish the task and make it pay.

In a larger business sense, your company may have a new project that it wants to tackle but doesn't quite have the funding for. In conversations with competitors, or via the messages it sends to its own customers, your company might indicate that such a market is unattractive, and that it's a time and money sink with no easy payoff.

But be aware, there is both an advantage and a danger in maneuvering for any key market position. When you set your entire organization in motion, you commit yourself. You become a force that can be noticed, analyzed, judged, and planned against. Others will react to you. If you bump against impediments to your progress, you may not attain your goal, while others will see where you were headed and get there first.

Think of your current products and your current market position as your base camps. This is your safe zone. If you abandon this safety to pursue a new goal against difficult challenges, you risk losing the safety of what you already have. You should not expose the safe zone in order to make gains. A smart general does not order his men into a forced march with little rest, nor does he order them to shed their armor to speed their journey. If he does, they will arrive tired and unprotected, with no time to survey the field. They may arrive first, but they will arrive at a great disadvantage—overtaxed and poorly able to defend. The whole organization is at risk because of this error in judgment, in the name of speed.

What you already have—the market space you previously controlled and the technological advantages that you possess—will be at great risk when you jeopardize all for a big gain.

You may be partially successful. Your best workers will stay late. They will do their part. They will help you build the shell of your next successful product. But this panicked push into new and untried waters will leave you with half your organization in one camp and half in another, and everyone will be stressed. You will lose whatever advantages you already have. Market space will be captured from you. Burnt-out employees will be absorbed by competitors. You may arrive at your destination, but your workers, your army, will be depleted, disorganized, desperate, and headed for the door. And even without the market pressures, it stands to reason that an organization that maneuvers too fast arrives without the proper equipment, bandwidth, and talent to tackle the tasks at hand.

Safety in Numbers—The Power of Partnerships

One great way to move fast without risking the corporate nest egg is to partner with others who know more about the new landscape than you do. They bring to you specific technologies and market knowledge. You must bring them something of equal value. You must offer other technologies—distribution, integration, marketing savvy, anything that will push the cause along to create an advantage for both of you. The word is synergy, and you must always be on the lookout for synergistic partners. Do not be worried about sharing a slice of the pie, because together you'll be able to grab a much bigger pie.

The large Web portals/search engines are a perfect example of companies that partner to find the best synergies. Yahoo, Lycos, and Excite started as search and indexing specialists. But it soon became apparent that growth on the Web was becoming a page view game. These companies realized that pointing people immediately off to other sites wasn't the best thing to do. They also realized they could enhance the search experience by learning what people were most often searching for, and offering those things on their own sites.

For example, breaking news items are always popular search terms. But search engines could not turn into international news services overnight. They lacked that expertise. Even if they wanted to make the investment to develop a news reporter and article-publishing infrastructure, ever-shifting online usage patterns might make such an effort a waste of time. Better to work with the experts and license the news content. News services like the Associated Press and Reuters brought expertise the search engines lacked. In turn, the search engines brought what big media companies lacked—aggregated audiences and traffic-driving muscle.

Synergy.

However, if you are not well acquainted with the abilities of your potential partners, it is best not to enter into alliances with them. Those who lack knowledge of marketplace conditions, or the specific technology you use, cannot conduct proper product development for your organization. Yes, you need a local guide as you move into a new landscape. But you need a guide you can trust, and who also understands your business, its limits, and its advantages. Take your time. Find the right local guide. Find the right provider and the right synergy. If you are not sure about a potential partner, start slowly. Participate in minor projects at first. Test the waters. If the partner's performance is in doubt, stick to a shared risk/shared reward scenario. Perhaps you will just split the revenue on the finished product, without promising a flat fee to each other. See how they perform. A partner must be a good fit, the best fit, as you move steadily and purposefully into your expanded market.

Secure the Advantage

Move when it is advantageous for you to move. Prepare for that move when the time is not yet right, so that you will be ready. Work to create change that will hasten your advantage. **The trick is to impose your will on your opponent, but not allow the opponent to make choices and impose his will on you.** The manager who sees the value in diversion, division, and proper timing will be victorious. This is what maneuvering in business means today.

When the time is right to move, and you are prepared, be swift. When you are moving toward your new goal, be majestic. Look like a company that is sure of itself, from your marketing materials to its offices. **Be sure of yourself, from the way you shake hands and look people in the eyes, to the way you look like you belong right where you are, even if you're in a stranger's office.** You know you have the people to accomplish a task, or you know where to find them. You are a company that knows the market, the technology, and the players. If you aren't, you'd better become that fast. Look like a winner, speak like an expert, work like a master, know your business, and win big.

When the time comes to take possession of the new space, or even the tools, people, and equipment you need for your efforts, be fierce. If you have to be because you did not create the space yourself, you are a plunderer. Accept that about yourself. You are desperately fighting to stay alive. Act accordingly. Show mercy only to those who recognize your mastery in this new game. They may be your allies as you work to displace the dominant player.

When you make a stand and fight for your share of resources, workers, and business, be as firm as the mountains. When you sense the time is not right, remain hidden. Be unfathomable and hazy, as if hidden in the caves of those mountains. And when you finally strike, strike like lightning. Command attention. Look powerful and capable. Eventually, you will gain territory. You will have a new market to serve. Defend your new strategic points. Weigh every new situation, plan, and plan again. Upgrade technologies if needed. Be ready, because you may have only one chance.

Here are some simple rules that can help you win market share and run circles around your opponents.

- By holding out advantages to an opponent, you can entice the opponent to approach you of his own accord. You then have an advantage for negotiations. Likewise, if you know what the opponent is attracted to, you can withhold it.

- If your opponent appears to be waiting and building strength for a big push, you can harass her. You can challenge her business plan to others, even to the press. You can also attempt to starve your opponent, taking away employees and business. You can force her to move and refocus on a different niche.

- Processing information is more cost-effective than moving physical products. Increasingly, the value of a company is found not in its physical possessions, but in its people and ideas. Your information-driven assets are your key weapons.

- Appear at points that your opponents must quickly defend. Offer to handle small projects for their best customers. Those customers might be very interested in testing you to judge your performance. Go to places where you aren't expected. Show up at trade shows and schmooze your opponents' best accounts.

- When you need to motivate your workers for a huge new project, sometimes it's better to do it in a nonstressful situation. Yes, competition can be a great motivator, but it can also cause burnout. Developing new products in a more relaxed situation, where time can be taken to get things right, has its advantages. It's like an army that can march slowly, away from the enemy. It can rest and prepare with little distress or distraction.

- Distance means very little any more. Geography plays less of a role in deciding who competes with whom. You have more opportunities, and more threats, than ever. Your competitors may also be your customers today because of the strange alliances you'll form to compete worldwide.

- Time is more important than ever. Instant interactivity is a must. The faster you can plug into someone else's supply chain, the faster you can grab new opportunities. Be able to restructure your process very quickly.

- Attack the weak points where you know you can win. Look for vulnerabilities where you know you have better products, technology, and people. On your end, don't hold on to positions or business where you know you aren't the best. You are only invulnerable if you know you are defending a strong position.

- Add value in whatever you do. You will be disintermediated if you do not. If your products help establish a platform or a business standard, you can buy a long-term market position. On the Net, value does not come from scarcity. The more plentiful your presence, the more muscle you acquire. Giving away your product may actually help you control a market, so that you can leverage business and profits in other ways.

- Look specifically for opponents who do not know how to defend well. Their business will be the easiest to take. You will grow and become a larger and more formidable opponent. Opponents will cast the same hungry eye on you, but if they don't know what to attack—your weak points—they will be less likely to attack at all. If they do attack, their lack of knowledge means they are less likely to choose the right target.

- Your people are your most important asset. Take care of them, especially if you have to work them hard. Allow them to share in the rewards of a big win. Offer the best rewards to your best workers.

- Not all middlemen will be disintermediated. Become an infomediary. These are people who not only connect buyers with sellers, but who enable information swaps that strengthen supply chain management. They turn raw data into usable information. They add value.

- Learn to be invisible unless you are making a big play. Your strengths and weaknesses, even your biggest projects, should remain hidden and unknown. If your enemy doesn't know you, you control the direction of your encounters.

- Every product and service has the potential to become a commodity where price is more important than minor product differences. Offering lower costs or unique services will help you survive. Relying on old-economy physical barriers like time and distance will place you at risk.

- Speed is of the essence when you do move. Move with confidence. If you need to retreat, do so before your opponent learns anything about your operations.

- Success is accelerated on the Web. Success spreads like wildfire. Be able to quickly ramp up to the next level when you do succeed.

- The world is moving away from bulk transactions toward one-to-one sales. Offering products that can be quickly customized for buyers can help you gain an edge.

- If you need to battle it out for market space, customers, media notice, and acknowledged leadership, you may find that your opponent doesn't allow a direct challenge, hiding behind the protection of a large organization. All you need to do is directly attack a piece of their business that they are obliged to defend or attack them in the press.

- If your opponent challenges you, and you don't feel the time is right, you can avoid the fight by throwing out something they don't expect, perhaps a new, but ultimately minor product, or start talking directly to their best customers, putting them on the defensive.

- By knowing what your opponent is working on, while they know nothing of your efforts, you can keep your efforts concentrated, while they must be divided.

- When your organization is unified against a single cause, while your opponent is fractured, you are more powerful, at least for your limited effort.

- The lag between desire and purchase of an item has closed, thanks to the Internet. All products are available all the time, anywhere. If you can close the gaps between knowing, finding, and purchasing, you have won a customer. The process of marketing, sales, and order fulfillment are merging.

- Do not let your enemy know what you will challenge or where the confrontation will take place. That is your strength. Your opponent will weaken some parts as he moves to strengthen others.

- There are strengths in numbers, even if you are the smaller organization. If the opponent has to prepare for numerous divergent projects, you have the numeric strength for the specific things you want to attack.

- Even if your opponent is larger, they might be prevented from attacking you if they don't know you, or know what to challenge.

- Still, rouse your opponent enough so you might learn something of them. Discover their plans and chances of success. Carefully compare your organizations, so that you may know where strength and weaknesses lie for each.

- Your opponent's own tactics can produce a victory for you if you know them, anticipate them, and allow your opponent to move in a way that you can understand and influence.

- As you work this way, others may notice your tactics. But they will not see the strategy you are using because it lies in the decisions you make based on your knowledge of both sides.

- Do not repeat tactics that have been successful once. Microsoft's usual tactics have not helped Bill Gates achieve victory in the Corbis/Getty face-off.

- Be like water running downhill. Rush toward the easy path to the easy win. Strike at the weak points. And, just as water molds to the ground over which it runs, you work out your victory in relation to the foe you are facing.

- There are no constant conditions. Modify your tactics in relation to your opponent and market conditions.

keep an eye on the new horizon

The best chess player, commander, or business leader has one crucial ability: to be able to feel the pulse of the future, to look beyond the battle at what looms on the horizon. In order to succeed in the e-world, you must be able to indulge in a vision of the future. Take advantage of opportunities and know how advancements in other areas might affect your business.

By now, we have all noticed the tremendous changes that have taken place to the world's communications systems. We all recognize the new competitive landscape we've entered and the challenges that lie ahead. What we don't know exactly is where we'll go from here. But we have some ideas.

The general direction is clear, though difficult to understand without looking down the road a full 20 years. Look that far out, and you'll realize that we are slowly entering the realm of science fiction. As the gee-whiz technologies of the past slowly morph into the realities of the future, the Internet, or whatever the Internet becomes, is slowly being integrated ever deeper into our lives and into our consciousness. Like electric lights, it will be everywhere—to the point where it becomes transparent and unnoticed. Throughout this integration, new opportunities will arise and new fortunes will be made.

Sometime in the next 10 years, the sprawling wonder that we know as the Internet will cease to exist. Yes, the name will live on, and so will the things we've come to love, like e-mail, Web pages, e-commerce functions, database access, and games. But the Internet itself will change. More efficient protocols will be hammered out to move data faster and more efficiently. Video and other multimedia will be embedded to the point where they become the main focus for many Net visitors. And the Net itself will fragment into thousands of virtual private networks. Rather than having free access to everything, people will pay small fees for access to specific information that's important to them, from video and music feeds to specialized business news and data. They will pay to access supply chain networks, set up on secure leased lines, for members only.

And we will even manage our own virtual private networks. These will be the networks that infiltrate every part of our home, from fuse box to phone lines, from light bulbs to coffeemaker. Through secure home networks, you will control everything in your home and customize the way you interact with the outside world.

The Internet will also fragment by device. No longer will you sit at a desk and surf everything on the Net. There will be one kind of Web on your desktop, networked games on your game console, and a heavily edited, streamlined Web for your cell phones and handheld devices. You'll have voice navigation on your telephone (with computer voices that read text messages). You'll have specialized multimedia interfaces for surfing digital entertainment content via your TV.

And specialty computers will start looking less like computers and more like the devices they are replacing. Already we've seen the Kerbango Internet Radio that looks just like a regular desktop radio except that you plug it into the Net. New VCRs come with hard drives instead of tapes and have the ability to capture not just TV shows but also streaming digital video if you have an Internet connection on your cable TV system.

This is the point where Net access and interaction starts to become ubiquitous. When it's in your lights, your TV, your appliances, and your bedroom, it's not really the Internet anymore. It's your life. And that's where the realm of science fiction comes in. With these tools, the possibilities are endless and so are the perils.

At the dawn of the new millennium, we stand on the brink of something so fantastic, that we dare not think of all the possible futures lurking before us. Some of these possible futures are bright, happy, and wonderful. Others, considering the capabilities of hackers, and considering how data can be used when collected in the right way, are dark, troubling, and violent. We need to choose one of those futures, and we fear we may choose incorrectly. We end up feeling like a deer caught in someone's headlights. We sense that something life-changing is coming. We know we should react. But we don't know which way to leap. Yet we don't want to just stand still either, watching the future bear down on us, waiting for the forces of change to make a life-altering decision for us.

Unfortunately, you can't predict the winning technologies or strategies for the next five years. But surprisingly, you can predict the path technology will take over the next 20 years. It's a path that has already been supposed. This knowledge can be found in the popular cyberpunk novels of the 1980s and 1990s. Novels by people like William Gibson (*Neuromancer, All Tomorrow's Parties*), Neal Stephenson (*Snow Crash, Cryptonomicon*), and Bruce Sterling (*Schismatrix, A Good Old-Fashioned Future*) have set out a path where many people think the future will lead.

These novels are actually silly, overblown, and far-fetched. And only parts of them deal with computer technologies. Yet they've made some stunning predictions that have proven true. For example, *Neuromancer*, in 1984, coined the term cyberspace and laid out the concept for virtual reality. Gibson has been mentioned as an inspiration by more than one developer of VR technologies. *Cryptonomicon* deals with data encryption and the need for protecting national and corporate secrets.

But the path these novels outline is clear. **We are moving toward a future where computer networks are our lifeblood.** We will interact with corporations, banks, and government mostly by interacting with data that these entities produce. The science of artificial intelligence will advance to the point where Net sites (let's not call them Web sites, since there will be so many ways to reach them) will anticipate our needs when we arrive. They will answer questions in plain language, step through routines for us, and even interact with other AI forms to work through preliminary levels for business development contact.

Embryonic Markets and Enormous Opportunities

While it's difficult to predict which technologies or companies will conquer a particular market niche, it's a bit easier to predict which markets will evolve in the next few years.

If we extrapolate current trends, here are some of the things we know will happen. It's not too late to become first mover in some of these new markets. But it's more likely that you won't have the luxury of arriving first at these battlefields. Instead, you'll need to judge your opponent and the lay of the land, and prepare to take these markets by hard work, cunning, and proper timing.

- **The Wonder and Aggravation of Wireless.** Mobile applications are not just another version of the Internet. By design, wireless applications must be small and fast. Stay away from any company trying to turn wireless devices into full Web browsers. The real goal for wireless is to identify the tiny editorial kernel of any new story, data trend, or mail message and send that kernel of information to the wireless user. The recipient can then decide whether more information is needed, and whether to receive that information via a wireless device or a desktop unit.

• *Business opportunity:* Boiled down data and news for easy delivery to wireless customers will flourish in the next few years. Cellular operators will offer IP packet data services at up to 144 Kbps by 2001, and even greater speeds two years after that, so the size of the delivered messages will creep up slightly.

Network managers face an increasing demand from employees to provide wireless access to company resources.

• *Business opportunity:* There is a great need for companies who can provide secure behind-the-firewall wireless access to internal data.

The trend toward merging voice and data on the same wireless devices is an integral part of what's driving the market for cellular systems. But standards are fragmented, and regulatory and frequency allocation issues are holding back deployment. Today's wireless data services are slow and rely on circuit switching. The WAP browsers in cell phones are limited by the network itself. New wireless technology is being deployed, but each of the three major digital cellular technologies, Time Division Multiple Access (TDMA), Code Division Multiple Access (CDMA), and Global System for Mobile Communications (GSM), has a different data strategy.

• *Business opportunity:* Help create and set the standards that will be widely adopted to solve the integration issues for all three services.

Bluetooth and future point-to-point technologies for wireless services will continue to drive handheld devices toward new uses. These include using your wireless device for point-of-purchase interaction. One hang-up for this is that credit card companies don't want to handle micropayments. But these are especially important for small purchases, or for rewards-based targeted advertising.

- *Business opportunity*: Finding a way to channel micropayments through credit card channels before telephone companies, which are experts in billing incrementally for pennies, can gain control of all wireless billing.

- **The Promise of Immersion Technologies.** For years, the Internet has offered a 3-D modeling language that allows programmers to create virtual spaces that visitors can literally walk through. It's called the Virtual Reality Modeling Language (VRML). Visitors to a VRML-enabled site need a special browser plug-in that lets them interpret a VRML scene, and navigate through rooms and around objects.

  But VRML has been little more than a novelty. People tend to visit VRML scenes once or twice, but they don't come back. You can't really do much in a primitive VR world. Managers of VRML sites usually noticed visitors would walk around a bit, and then find someone to chat with. And they did so in traditional text chat. Who needs a bandwidth-heavy VR world to do text chat? Visitors would also walk around to view graphics, visit hyperlinks, or listen to embedded music. All these things could be accomplished without a 3-D interface.

  - *Business opportunity*: Construct a truly useful and compelling 3-D meeting space that users will want to visit again and again. Worlds.com may come the closest today, but it's very chat and socially oriented. What about a 3-D space where machine parts can be viewed, revolved, tested, and purchased? Vios (www.vios .com) has perhaps the highest resolution 3-D space (it's shipped on a CD-ROM), but it's not heavily populated to date.

  While VRML has foundered, peripheral VR technologies have continued to evolve. Cyber goggles, which used to be clunky, four-pound, 10-inch-deep scopes that strapped to your head, have evolved into elegant solutions like Sony's Glasstron glasses that weigh just 3.5 ounces. With their half-inch-deep screen, Glasstron lenses look like little more than extra-thick sunglasses. On the inside, the view looks like a 52-inch color monitor hovering about 6 feet away.

- *Business opportunity:* Heads-up display with real-time motion capture and position tracker with data feedback. Such systems have existed for quite a while as kludged-together arrangements used by NASA and others to provide immersive VR environments. But no one has yet built a mass-marketed system that incorporates inexpensive hardware like the Glasstron glasses. This could be a home run for someone who puts all the pieces together in a turnkey system that could be used over the Internet.

Haptic interfaces like SenseAble Technologies' Phantom systems allow people to reach out and feel objects that appear on a Web page. These interact with Web objects that contain data enabling a force-feedback mechanism in the haptic interface. The Phantom unit includes a finger thimble mounted on a special arm attached to a desktop and plugged into a computer. If there is, for example, a vase on screen, you can touch it, feel its curves, and even place your hand inside, feeling the inner walls. More information on haptic devices can be found at haptic.mech .northwestern.edu/.

- *Business opportunities:* Reduce the cost of a haptic interface from several hundred dollars to about the cost of a mouse, then mass market it to computer manufacturers who could ship it with all new units. Be a content provider who produces Web objects that can be felt by haptic users and integrated on standard Web pages. Think of the plethora of haptic applications that could be built for the online adult industry.

With all these neat peripherals, some people expect VRML to make a comeback, especially as higher bandwidth makes it easier to download VRML scenes. But it may be too late for VRML to be a leading technology for 3-D spaces. Already, computer games offer very realistic worlds that use other methods to generate the illusion of a 3-D space. Also, there is also a new componentized Next-Generation specification for Web3D that may replace VRML. It includes X3D, an XML-capable architecture and process for encoding data. VRML's days may be numbered, but it gave us a grand start down the road toward immersive Internet spaces.

- **The Continued Rise of Game Consoles.** The other computer in many households isn't a traditional desktop unit or laptop. Instead, it's a computer game console plugged into a television set. We've all heard of Nintendo 64, Sony Playstation, and Sega Dreamcast. But the public at large hasn't paid much attention to the fact that many of these consoles now ship with built-in Internet access. This is a threat to the notion of a desktop unit as the main way to cruise the Net. *Boardwatch* magazine has warned its subscribers, who are mostly small ISPs, that Sega, Sony, and Nintendo are their new competition.

What these units provide is a totally different way of interacting over the Internet. Web browsers are not needed. Instead, these computers immerse their users in a game interface, allowing users to battle or interact with other players who are networked within the same game. Beyond this, links can be embedded in games that allow visitors to jump to other games and other specialized areas. With minor modifications, these game consoles can be integrated with the immersion hardware previously mentioned, creating a full-contact method for interacting with other players. The game console in your family room has the potential to be as powerful and popular as your desktop computer. This is an extremely new phenomenon with no clear first mover for several parts of this marketplace.

- *Business opportunities:* Yes, we know who the game console manufacturers are. But who will build the communities that will draw the players in and create the first real Gibson-like cyber world? Will there be a search engine equivalent for game consoles? Will haptic objects be created and shared to the point where they proliferate throughout game sites? Beyond gaming, can these consoles be used to view other types of data? Perhaps you could walk through a 3-D representation of the current weather, or through the day's stock ticker, viewing prices and volume data from all sides.

Sega is trying to corner a new type of ISP market by offering SegaNet, an online gaming service for Dreamcast players. The core product is SegaSports, with shared sports games. Besides offering a network connection, it also offers a sense of identity and community for players. That's a good way to combat the stereotype of isolation associated with online gaming.

- *Business opportunities:* Established ISPs should be equipped to offer services similar to SegaNet. Other search and community-building efforts should follow. Creating a new market niche specifically for gaming and entertainment, using gaming consoles as an entry point, could be a huge market for anyone daring enough to make an investment in this new market.

- **A Mass Market for Multimedia.** The only thing protecting the movie industry today from file sharing and pirating is that the file sizes are too large to move easily around the Net. But since bandwidth is doubling every six to 12 months, file size will become irrelevant and copying and sharing movies will be common. Encryption and single-view licensing will offer some protection, but hackers will always be able to break the protections. A balance of sorts will be reached when a license to view the movie is cheap enough that breaking the encryption will seem like too much trouble.

- *Business opportunities:* Be able to serve digital video with an economy of scale that only requires you to make pennies on each delivery. Be able to provide good, but cheap, digital encryption for streaming video that's just tough enough to hack so most people won't bother. Be an ASP for digital content hosting, or for digital editing tools used by the entertainment industry.

- **The Rebirth of Free Services.** Free ISP service is the most noteworthy of the free access movements that gained acceptance in the late 1990s. But in theory, many things are free on the Net. Just let the banner ads load, and you can read free news, watch free video streams, play free games, and more. Games and news will survive. But things like free ISP will only survive if they're able to establish the proper revenue model and sales force. The first round of free Internet access seems to have failed miserably. But the failure did not come from a lack of customers. Most free ISPs had all the subscribers they could handle. Where they dropped the ball was the way they sold ads. They collected substantial demographic information for their subscribers, but they didn't take advantage of it. They didn't have sales forces capable of selling and targeting ads in a way that boosted the value of those ads. Trade magazine publishers will tell you how difficult it is to find salespeople who can target a specific market segment. You need a person with a lot of industry contacts and a Rolodex full of numbers. Even then, it's a challenge for that salesperson to sell highly expensive ads in a highly targeted publication.

Providers of free Internet dial-up services could never employ enough industry-expert salespeople to take advantage of all the demographic information they had about their customers. Even if they know their subscriber base includes, say 55 veterinarians, 92 car salesmen, and 115 computer programmers, the free service can't employ enough salespeople with knowledge of the top advertiser prospects in all these divergent markets. The logistics of making targeted advertising work in a free dial-up service seem to be insurmountable.

- *Business opportunity:* Free Net access may survive by blending with other services. What if the provider of a free Internet service didn't have to worry about selling ads at all? They could partner with dozens of trade publications that could offer their own flavor of the free ISP. These trade publications are already experts at selling targeted advertising for niche markets. They could sell targeted ads for the free veterinarian ISP or the free car dealer ISP, splitting the ad revenue with the Internet dial-up access provider.

  Other free services may survive by providing associated fee-based services. The free, open-source Linux OS has spawned several companies who make their money via consulting, troubleshooting, and maintenance.

- **The Rise of Peer-to-Peer Technologies.** These are services that enable computers to access the local hard drives of other computers connected to the same service. Napster is a peer-to-peer technology. People share music files from their hard drives with no Web server as a middleman.

  - *Business opportunities:* Instead of just music, this type of service could be set up for many types of files. Bits of code used by programmers. Term papers. Computer aided design (CAD) files. The trick will be to monotize such efforts.

- **The Potential of Interactive Advertising.** Future generations of advertising on the Web will be increasingly interactive. Thanks to the multimedia capabilities of broadband, ads will be more television-like in appearance. But they'll be better targeted, and carry a call to action for the recipients—such as an invitation to obtain a specific product or service that the system knows the recipient has been seeking. The content of the ads will be targeted at specific users, containing moving graphics, music, links, and pull-down menus specifically selected for the recipient's tastes. Recipients can be tracked so that, even if they remain anonymous, statistics about them can be collected and used to generate profiles.

- *Business opportunities:* There will be an increase in reward-based commercials incorporating challenges in which the viewer can win prizes targeted to them, while being exposed to select brands. (Thus the need for the micropayment solution previously mentioned.) In the case of games, the game can be interrupted for a commercial. The player will have to watch the short commercial before returning to the game at the point where it was interrupted. Ads will also take the form of free demo versions of games, music, and videos. Just like today's game arcades in malls, where kids can view demo versions of games until they decide what to play, view-only ad versions of games can keep viewers interested until they decide what to try. Viewers may choose to pay a small fee and skip the commercials.

- **E-mail—Rescued from Spam and Rebuilt as an Opt-In Powerhouse.** The UCLA Internet Report, *Surveying the Digital Future,* found that over two-thirds of people in the United States now have access to the Internet, and 42 percent send e-mail daily. Nine percent of the people send e-mail hourly. That could add up to over four trillion e-mail messages per year. (The U.S. Postal Service delivers about 100 billion pieces of mail annually.) But how many of those e-mail messages are actually read? Spam is such a problem that most serious Net cruisers have a half-dozen dummy mailboxes set up to catch spam and keep it away from their main address (which is closely protected).

  - *Business opportunities:* Continued development of spam-filtering software that lets users choose what messages they will see. Continued development of opt-in services for special interests, helping those who do want mail to find newsletters and ad services that are a perfect mix for them. As bandwidth increases to most homes, create multimedia mail services with news, weather, and sports content.

All these evolving markets have the potential to grow as large as the most popular Net services today. Get in early, and you may catch a remarkable wave. Know what's coming and you will be on the cutting edge. The trick will be surviving, knowing your competition, and anticipating their actions.

Future Imperfect

During the next few years, Net-based empires will rise and crumble. Innocent people will be caught in the crossfire as companies battle for technological and market supremacy. Careers will be ruined. Families will break up. New economies and currencies will be born, run their course, and collapse. These events will be no different from the business life-cycle trajectories we see in the real world, but they may move faster and be more brutal in their execution.

> The Internet is indeed a war zone, but it is not a place to be feared. It is a vibrant democracy.
>
> Yet the same principles that have shaped the world will continue to shape the Net. Laws will be made. Laws will be broken. People will flee across new types of borders to avoid new types of laws.

But the Net itself remains amoral, just as real-world weapons have no particular morality. The moral issues come from how weapons are used—offensively or defensively. Weapons can be used to protect, serve, and build, or they can be used to destroy and thwart the will of others. The Net is no different.

The Internet is a unique world upon which we build a set of communities that are as virtuous, or as villainous, as humans care to make them. Sun Tzu fought for political leaders and represented their interests. However, in spite of representing a specific political viewpoint, his writings indicate that he felt goodness and fairness, as he understood it, should prevail in the world. One of the main reasons he wrote *The Art of War* was to ensure that those who enter battles, and who have a sense of right and wrong, might have the knowledge and tools they need for success.

Do not underestimate the good, or the bad, that can be done through the Internet. The Net is simply what it is. What we make from it as it grows, and as it becomes ever more intertwined with our lives, is up to us. Business is business, and there will be many battles along the way. Those who understand *The Art of .combat,* and those who fight a good fight for a respectable cause, will win those battles.

The optimist likes to believe that good will prevail and that new tools or weapons will be used for the proper causes. If that doesn't happen, the optimist also hopes that good people will work together to fix whatever has gone wrong. If this is true, then the Internet should be able to fix itself when things get off track. Thus, the best is yet to come for the Net, or whatever the Internet becomes.

It is the promise of the future. It is the home of the brave.

index

Melrose Public Library
Melrose, MA

GAYLORD M